Summer 1998

||||||||||||||||||| D1055999

COLLECTOR'S
VALUE GUIDE™

Collector Handbook and Price Guide

Ty® Beanie Babies®

Collector's Name

Contents

Ty® Beanie Babies®

COLLECTOR'S VALUE GUIDE™ and THE COLLECTOR'S POCKET PLANNER™ are trademarks of Collectors' Publishing Co., Inc. The Collector's Value Guide™ is not affiliated with Ty Inc. or any of its affiliates, subsidiaries, distributors or representatives. Any opinions expressed are solely those of the authors, and do not necessarily reflect those of Ty Inc. Ty® and Beanie Babies® are registered trademarks of Ty Inc. Teenie Beanie Babies™, Pillow Pals™ and Attic Treasures Collection™ are trademarks of Ty Inc. Product names and product designs are the property of Ty Inc., Oakbrook, IL. Illustrations are the original creations and property of Collectors' Publishing Co., Inc.

Front cover foreground (left to right): Rocket™ and Whisper™.
Front cover background (left to right): Tracker™, Fortune™, Stinger™, Jake™ and Early™.
Back cover (left to right): Pinchers™, Bubbles™ and Rex™.

Managing Editor:	Jeff Mahony	Art Director:	Joe T. Nguyen
	jeff@collectorspub.com		*joe@collectorspub.com*
Associate Editors:	Melissa Bennett	Production Supervisor:	Scott Sierakowski
	Jan Cronan	Staff Artists:	Lance Doyle
	Gia C. Manalio		Kimberly Eastman
Editorial Assistants:	K. Nicole LeGard		Ryan Falis
	Scarlet H. Riley		David Ten Eyck
Contributing Editor:	Mike Micciulla		

Illustrations by David Ten Eyck.

ISBN 1-888914-28-9

COLLECTOR'S VALUE GUIDE™ is a trademark of Collectors' Publishing Co., Inc.
Copyright© by Collectors' Publishing Co., Inc. 1998.
All rights reserved. No part of this book may be reproduced or transmitted in any form or by any means, electronic or mechanical, including photocopying, recording, or by any information storage or retrieval system, without the written permission of the publisher.

Collectors' Publishing Co., Inc.
598 Pomeroy Avenue
Meriden, CT 06450
www.collectorspub.com

INTRODUCING THE COLLECTOR'S VALUE GUIDE™

*W*elcome to the Summer 1998 Edition of the *Beanie Babies® Value Guide!* Who would have guessed that those adorable beanbag critters that were introduced to the world as toys, would grow to be one of the best-selling collectibles in history! Ty® Beanie Babies have created a collecting frenzy and as more people are discovering them, more and more questions about Beanies are being asked. So, whether you're a passionate collector or a casual fan, the Collector's Value Guide™ provides all the latest Beanie Babies information:

- New May Releases & Retirements
- Larger-Than-Ever Color Photos
- Up-To-Date Secondary Market Values For Each Generation Tag
- Everything You Need To Know About Your Beanies, Including Poems, In One Spot
- The 10 Most Valuable Beanies
- In-Depth Look at Hang Tags & Tush Tags
- New Teenie Beanies Information
- Room To Record The Value Of Your Own Beanie Collection
- Variations & Name Changes
- Fun & Games
- An Overview Of Other Ty Plush Lines
- See The First Winners Of The "Create Your Own Dream Beanie Contest"

The Collector's Value Guide now makes collecting Beanie Babies more fun than ever!

*I*t's probably safe to say that the term "Beanie Babies" has taken its place among such other common household terms like BARBIE™ and Mr. Potato Head®. By now, just about everyone in America (and in many other countries, as well) has heard of these irresistible beanbag toys. The innocent-looking plush animals and mythical creatures have taken the world by storm, and the frenzy has shown no signs of subsiding!

IN THE BEGINNING . . .

The Beanie Babies success story is certainly one for the record books. Ty Inc. of Oakbrook, Illinois has been producing under-stuffed, handmade plush animals since the mid-1980s. Founded by H. Ty Warner, the privately-owned toy manufacturer eventually decided to create a line of reasonably-priced beanbag animals – the spark that ignited the Beanie Babies phenomenon.

TIME TO MAKE THE BEANIES . . .

Handmade in Korea or China, each Beanie begins its life as a piece of soft, plush material. A pattern is cut and sewn, and the newly-created form is then filled with small round polyvinyl chloride (P.V.C.) or polyethylene (P.E.) pellets. This special "weighted" filling that is sewn into each Beanie allows it to be posed into different positions. When it comes to the filling process, less is definitely more! Leaving some extra room is what gives these toys their playful floppiness.

Ty Inc. wanted to introduce children to animals from all around the world, and to do so at prices kids could afford. In 1994, the "Original Nine" Beanie Babies made their world debut at small retail stores in America. Today, many Beanies can still be found for $5 to $10 in the United States, Canada and Great Britain.

THE ATTRACTION . . .

After Beanie Babies hit store shelves in 1994, their popularity gradually took hold. By 1996, the plush creations were becoming a hot collectible, and so began the biggest craze since Cabbage Patch Dolls.

What is it about these little creatures that has made them virtually irresistible? At first glance, one would have to agree that they are extremely cute! Whether you prefer realistic-looking animals such as "Tuffy" the terrier or the playfully imaginative "Magic" the dragon, there is sure to be at least one that will capture your heart! What was your favorite animal when you were younger? A whale? A koala? A giraffe? Whichever animal you had a fondness for, it's a good bet that it's among Ty's Beanie Babies Collection!

Although Beanie Babies were originally intended as children's playthings, many adults are discovering these critters are good companions as well. Don't be surprised to find them sitting atop your coworkers' computers or riding in your neighbors' cars. Their undeniable playfulness and heartwarming faces can be pleasant reminders of simpler, less-stressful times!

MEANWHILE, ON THE WEB . . .

Beanie Babies have enjoyed immense popularity despite the fact that Ty has done virtually no advertising! The Internet is largely responsible for the craze surrounding these stuffed toys. In addition to Ty's own website (*www.ty.com*), numerous other sites have since cropped up, providing Beanie collectors with a wealth of resources for all the latest in Beanie Babies news and gossip.

While Ty Inc. has avoided advertising for the most part, other organizations have filled in the gaps. Countless books, magazines, newsletters and promotions have helped collectors become more aware of the latest happenings in the Beanie Babies world.

THEN CAME THE TEENIES . . .

While the Beanie Babies frenzy was already well underway in early 1997, the phenomenon received another boost in April 1997 from the McDonald's Teenie Beanie Babies promotion. McDonald's offered miniature versions of Beanie Babies in 10 different styles at participating restaurants, one free with each Happy Meal purchase. The response was so overwhelming that supplies ran out at many restaurants long before the five-week promotion officially ended! The promotion received a lot of media attention and inspired many new Beanie collectors.

In May 1998, Ty and McDonald's repeated its successful promotion in the United States and Canada, this time with twice as many Teenie Beanie Babies in 12 new styles. These tiny Beanies – again licensed by Ty but produced by an independent McDonald's supplier – were slated to be available for four weeks, but once again, the collecting frenzy depleted supplies quickly!

TAKE ME OUT TO THE BALLGAME . . .

Ty Inc. hit another grand slam with collectors when it agreed to give away a series of promotional Beanie Babies at sporting events. The first Beanie up to bat was "Cubbie," who stole hearts (not bases!) at the May 18, 1997 Chicago Cubs game.

In 1998, the company teamed up with 11 baseball teams and three basketball teams as a way to get kids and their families to the ballparks and basketball arenas.

MOVE OVER BABE!

"Valentino" the bear has become the first Beanie Babies animal to be displayed at the Baseball Hall of Fame in Cooperstown, New York. "Valentino" was the Beanie Babies giveaway at Yankee Stadium on May 17, 1998 when Yankee David Wells pitched a rare perfect game. "Valentino" joined Wells' hat and a ticket stub from the game in the Hall of Fame's 1998 highlights exhibit.

A MATTER OF SUPPLY AND DEMAND . . .

The popularity and staying power of Beanie Babies has gone beyond mere cuteness. These simple plush toys designed for children have become one of the newest and biggest collectible items on the market.

Part of Ty Inc.'s marketing strategy has been to limit the availability of the plush toys. They are not available through most large retail chains that typically carry stuffed animals. Rather, they are found in smaller toy, gift and card shops. The limited supply serves to fuel the demand as collectors realize they must have those elusive Beanies! In addition to this, Beanie Babies have been retired regularly since 1995, sending fans and collectors scurrying to find them before they are completely unobtainable.

THE PASSION CONTINUES . . .

Today, many collectors are trying to scout out special promotional Beanie Babies, as well as the more rare and older Beanies, to add to their growing collections. Collectors are constantly on the lookout for subtle differences that make their Beanies unique. For example, "Princess," the bear that honors the late Princess Diana, has been issued with both polyvinyl chloride (P.V.C.) and polyethylene (P.E.) pellets and die-hard collectors want both versions!

One of the most elusive of all Beanies is the limited edition bear that Ty gave to its sales representatives and employees in December 1996. Each of the "new face" violet teddy bears came with a red tush tag and no hang tag. Only 300 to 400 were produced, making them exceptionally hard to find.

A WORD ABOUT TAGS . . .

An important factor in the world of collecting Beanie Babies is the hang tag that comes attached to each animal. These red and white heart-shaped tags have undergone several changes (see pages 15-17 for more details), but the bottom line is that to many collectors these tags are just as important as the animals themselves! The absence of a tag can reduce the secondary market value of your Beanie Babies by as much as 50%! Should you decide to give the toy to a young child, however, it's best to remove the tags for safety.

MISTAGGED BEANIES

Errors on the Ty hang tags and tush tags are a fairly common occurrence. Some collectors are willing to pay a little more for Beanies with mistakes that help pinpoint the production date of a Beanie, such as the recent switched tags on "Iggy" and "Rainbow" (or "Echo" and "Waves"). However, these errors are considered by many collectors to be "mistakes" as opposed to "variations" and, to this point, they have not seen a significant increase in value on the secondary market.

BEWARE OF COUNTERFEIT BEANIES . . .

Altered and counterfeit Beanies began invading the Beanie scene in 1996 by people hoping to take advantage of new and inexperienced collectors. It is best for collectors who want to buy old or rare Beanies to become as educated as possible about what the product should look like and cost – before the purchase takes place!

WHERE DOES IT GO FROM HERE . . .

While no one can predict the future of Beanie Babies, one thing is clear: Beanies are downright adorable and will continue to delight children and adults for years. Isn't that what Beanie Babies were meant to do all along?

*T*t's now clear that when Ty honored 28 Beanie Babies with retirement this May, it was to make room for the 14 new releases that were introduced on May 30, 1998. Here's a look at the wonderful new members of the Beanie Babies family!

Ants™ . . . This gray fellow is starving and there's no snout (I mean, doubt) about it, he's on the search for something to fill his tummy. But there's no reason to be afraid, even if you're an ant or even an aunt, the only thing that this Beanie is hungry for is a little love.

Early™ . . . A sure sign of spring (and quite appropriately the spring releases), this robin sings his song of the season from the depths of his bright red belly. And as he is one of the first of his kind, it will have to be the early bird who catches this Beanie as he is sure to fly off store shelves quickly.

Fetch™ . . . This golden pooch has been waiting all season for the warm weather to come so he can go out into the yard and play his favorite game. And with a name like "Fetch," there's no confusion about what game that is.

Fortune™ . . . Collectors who missed out on their chance to add the retired "Peking" to their collections will find themselves fortunate to have another opportunity to purchase such a unique type of bear. This spiffy panda, decked out with a red ribbon around his neck, is bound to bring peace, love and happiness to anyone who owns him.

Gigi™ . . . This canine femme fatale looks prim and proper with her shiny black coat and red ribbons on her ears. Sure to be well-liked by the other Beanie dogs, this little beauty dresses up any collection, no bones about it.

Glory™ . . . Let's hear it for the red, white and blue! Covered with red and blue stars and sporting an American flag on her chest, "Glory" is sure to shine in the hearts of every American with her adorable display of patriotism. To top it all off, "Glory" shares her country's birthday, July 4th!

Jabber™ . . . It's hard to tell what's louder, the vivid shades of this very colorful bird or the sound of his jabbering voice. Nevertheless, this striking Beanie has something to say and will be able to sweet-talk his way into any collection.

Jake™ . . . It's duck season again and Beanie lovers will be out hunting down the first mallard duck to swim into the Beanie pond. Yet this adorable little drake has nothing to worry about, the only thing that these Beanie hunters will be scouring the fields and ponds with is love.

Kuku™ . . . Bird-watchers will go "cuckoo" for this unique feathery friend. The regal "Kuku," a cockatoo with a puffy crown on his head, is ready to spread his wings and soar into the Beanie kingdom.

Rocket™ . . . "Rocket" darts into the skies of
the Beanie Babies collection chirping the
perfect pitch of the spring season. As one
of the first members of his species to be
introduced, this blue jay is sure to score
with collectors.

Stinger™ . . . If you happen to come across this
sharp little guy when turning over
rocks or you feel something crawling
up your arm, don't be afraid, it's only
"Stinger." And the only sting you
may feel is the sting in your heart if
you don't catch this unusual critter
before he scampers out of stores.

Tracker™ . . . Don't let those sad puppy dog
eyes fool you, this pudgy pooch "nose"
exactly what he's doing. With his floppy
ears and his pleasant manner, "Tracker" will
track down the pathway to your heart.

Whisper™ . . . Prancing lightly into
the Beanie collection, "Whisper" is
like a soft summer breeze.
However, as she is the first deer in
the Beanie Forest, it is unlikely that
her arrival will be quite that quiet.

Wise™ . . . It sure was wise of this feathered
friend to glide into the Beanie forest to take over
as the voice of wisdom, as his distant cousin
"Hoot" has recently retired from the position.
Sporting a mortarboard in honor of his graduating class, this Beanie is sure to hold the honor of
being the top of his class – and just in time for
graduation season.

TEENIE BEANIE BABIES™ COME AND GO

Last year, Ty and McDonald's introduced a "Teenie Beanie Babies" promotion that was to become a collector feeding frenzy of sorts. People traveled to every McDonald's restaurant within driving distance to feast their eyes on these Teenie Beanies. Based on this success, Ty and McDonald's decided to do it again, starting on May 22, 1998.

This time, McDonald's offered 12 Beanies to fill that collector appetite, all of which are "teenie" replications of their Beanie Babies counterparts. The offerings included "Doby" the Doberman, "Bongo" the monkey, "Twigs" the giraffe, "Inch" the inchworm, "Pinchers" the lobster, "Happy" the hippo, "Mel" the koala, "Scoop" the pelican, "Bones" the dog, "Zip" the cat, "Waddle" the penguin and "Peanut" the elephant. Despite the fact that about twice as many Teenie Beanies were distributed during this promotion than in the first, these little stuffed toys sold out quickly.

CLUB "MEMBERS ONLY" BEAR ANNOUNCED

In celebration of the first year of the Beanie Babies Official Club, Ty announced on May 1 that it will offer "Clubby" the bear to all club members. Now, not only will members be the envy of everyone on their block as privileged members of the club, they will also be honored as exclusive owners of this adorable Beanie bear. No Beanie fan will want to miss the opportunity to purchase this bear for only $5.99 (plus shipping and handling), as he is limited to one per club member and is sure to be a very special addition to any collection.

*T*y announced the largest retirement to date on May 1, 1998, on its website (*www.ty.com*). The retirement announcement included 28 Beanie Babies, comprising about one-third of all current Beanies at the time. Here's a complete list of all the officially retired Beanie Babies with their animal type and issue year.

INTRODUCING THE MAY 1, 1998 RETIREMENTS!

Baldy™. . . . . . . *eagle, 1997*
Blizzard™ . . . . . . *tiger, 1997*
Bones™. . . . . *dog, 1994*
Ears™ . . . . *rabbit, 1996*
Echo™ . . . . . . *dolphin, 1997*
Floppity™ . . . . . *bunny, 1997*
Gracie™ . . . . *swan, 1997*
Happy™ . . . . *hippo, 1994*
Hippity™ . . . . . . *bunny, 1997*
Hoppity™ . . . . . *bunny, 1997*
Inch™ . . . . . *inchworm, 1995*
Inky™. . . . . . . *octopus, 1994*
Jolly™ . . . . *walrus, 1997*
Lucky™ . . . . . *ladybug, 1994*

Patti™ . . . . . . *platypus, 1994*
Peanut™ . . . . *elephant, 1995*
Pinchers™ . . . . *lobster, 1994*
Quackers™ . . . . . *duck, 1994*
Rover™. . . . . *dog, 1996*
Scottie™. *Scottish terrier, 1996*
Squealer™ . . . . *pig, 1994*
Stripes™ . . . . *tiger, 1995*
Twigs™ . . . . . . *giraffe, 1996*
Waddle™ . . . . *penguin, 1995*
Waves™ . . . . . . *whale, 1997*
Weenie™ . . *dachshund, 1996*
Ziggy™ . . . . *zebra, 1995*
Zip™ . . . . *cat, 1994*

A dozen new Teenie Beanie Babies were available at McDonald's restaurants in May 1998. As with the April 1997 Teenie Beanie sell out, the 1998 promotion was a success! All 12 of the Teenies were sold out by June 12, 1998 (and earlier in many places). The 12 new retirements are: "Bones," "Bongo," "Doby," "Happy," "Inch," "Mel," "Peanut," "Pinchers," "Scoop," "Twigs," "Waddle" and "Zip."

RETIRED DECEMBER 31, 1997

1997 Teddy™ . . . *bear, 1997*
Bucky™ . . . . . . *beaver, 1996*
Cubbie™ . . . . *bear, 1994*
Goldie™. . . . . *goldfish, 1994*
Lizzy™ . . . . *lizard, 1995*

Magic™. . . . . . *dragon, 1995*
Nip™ . . . . *cat, 1994*
Snowball™. . *snowman, 1997*
Spooky™ . . . . . . *ghost, 1995*

RETIRED OCTOBER 1, 1997

Ally™ . . . . . . *alligator, 1994*
Bessie™ . . . . *cow, 1995*
Flip™ . . . . *cat, 1996*
Hoot™ . . . . *owl, 1996*
Legs™ . . . . *frog, 1994*
Seamore™ . . . . . . *seal, 1994*

Speedy™ . . . . . . *turtle, 1994*
Spot™ . . . . *dog, 1994*
Tank™ . . . . . *armadillo, 1996*
Teddy™ (brown) . *bear, 1994*
Velvet™ . . . . . *panther, 1995*

RETIRED MAY 11, 1997

Bubbles™ . . . . *fish, 1995*
Digger™ . . . . *crab, 1994*
Flash™ . . . . . . *dolphin, 1994*
Garcia™. . . . . *bear, 1996*
Grunt™ . . . . *razorback, 1996*

Manny™ . . . . *manatee, 1996*
Radar™ . . . . *bat, 1995*
Sparky™ . . . *dalmatian, 1996*
Splash™. . . . . . . *whale, 1994*

RETIRED JANUARY 1, 1997

Chops™. . . . . *lamb, 1996*
Coral™ . . . . *fish, 1995*
Kiwi™ . . . . *toucan, 1995*
Lefty™ . . . . . . *donkey, 1996*
Libearty™. . . . . . *bear, 1996*

Righty™ . . . . *elephant, 1996*
Sting™ . . . . . . *stingray, 1995*
Tabasco™ . . . . *bull, 1995*
Tusk™ . . . . *walrus, 1995*

**OUT OF
PRODUCTION!**
Brownie™
Doodle™
Nana™
These Beanie
Babies were
renamed, therefore
they were never
officially retired.
That doesn't make
them any easier to
find however!

RETIRED JUNE 15, 1996

Bronty™ *brontosaurus, 1995*
Bumble™ . . . . *bee, 1995*
Caw™. . . . . *crow, 1995*

Flutter™. . . . . *butterfly, 1995*
Rex™ . . *tyrannosaurus, 1995*
Steg™. . . . *stegosaurus, 1995*

RETIRED JANUARY 7, 1996

Chilly™ . . . *polar bear, 1994*
Peking™. . . . . . *panda, 1994*
Teddy™
(cranberry) . . . . . . *bear, 1994*
Teddy™ (jade) . . *bear, 1994*

Teddy™
(magenta) . . . . *bear, 1994*
Teddy™ (teal) . . . *bear, 1994*
Teddy™ (violet). . *bear, 1994*
Web™ . . . . *spider, 1994*

RETIRED JUNE 15, 1995

Humphrey™ . . . *camel, 1994*
Slither™ . . . . . . *snake, 1994*

Trap™. . . . . *mouse, 1994*

*O*nce upon a time, shoppers brought their new Beanie Babies home, cut off the tags and tossed the tags away. But that was before Beanie Babies became a household word. Collectors now know that the tags are not only supposed to stay on the Beanies, but in fact can enhance their values.

Those who want to sell their Beanie Babies on the secondary market take care to see that each Beanie Babies animal is in mint condition, with both hang and tush tags intact. Some Beanie enthusiasts are also interested in determining the age of their Beanies using the bits of information available on the tags. There are now five recognized generations of hang tags and four versions of tush tags. A serious collector might prefer to have a "Squealer" or "Patti" with a first generation tag because these Beanie Babies are older than their newer namesakes with 5th generation tags.

THE DIFFERENT HANG TAGS . . .

1 Generation 1 (Early 1994 to Mid 1994): Beanie Babies first appeared with a double-sided, heart-shaped red tag. A slim "ty" logo outlined in gold adorned the front of the tag, while the Beanie's name and style number, as well as company information, was on the back.

The Beanie Babies Collection
Brownie ™ style 4010
© 1993 Ty Inc. Oakbrook, IL. USA
All Rights Reserved. Caution:
Remove this tag before giving
toy to a child. For ages 5 and up.
Handmade in Korea.
Surface
Wash.

2 Generation 2 (Mid 1994 to Early 1995): This was the first double tag that opened like a book. Inside was the Beanie's name and the style number, "To/From" for gift giving, reference to "The Beanie Babies Collection," and company information.

The Beanie Babies Collection
© 1993 Ty Inc. Oakbrook IL. USA
All Rights Reserved. Caution:
Remove this tag before giving
toy to a child. For ages 3 and up.
Handmade in China
Surface
Wash.

Chilly ™ style 4012
to _____
from _____
with
love

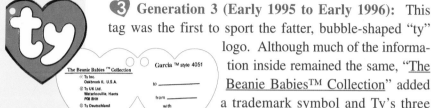

③ Generation 3 (Early 1995 to Early 1996): This tag was the first to sport the fatter, bubble-shaped "ty" logo. Although much of the information inside remained the same, "The Beanie Babies™ Collection" added a trademark symbol and Ty's three corporate addresses were included.

④ Generation 4 (Early 1996 to Late 1997): The front of the hang tag was again transformed with the addition of a yellow star and the words "Original Beanie Baby." On the inside, the 4th generation tag featured the popular Beanie birthdays and poems for the first time, as well as Ty's website information.

⑤ Generation 5 (Late 1997 to Current): At the end of 1997, the inside text was changed to a different type face. The date of birth is written out (February 13, 1995 instead of 2-13-95), the Internet address is abbreviated and the Beanie's style number has been deleted. Finally, the phrase "The Beanie Babies Collection®" is now registered (®), and the trademark symbol (™) has been dropped.

HANG TAG HISTORY – AT A GLANCE

Generation 1 – ❶ – Early 1994 to Mid 1994

Generation 2 – ❷ – Mid 1994 to Early 1995

Generation 3 – ❸ – Early 1995 to Early 1996

Generation 4 – ❹ – Early 1996 to Late 1997

Generation 5 – ❺ – Late 1997 to Current

COLLECTOR'S
VALUE GUIDE™

AND THE TUSH TAGS . . .

Also known as "body tags," cloth tush tags are sewn into the seams near the bottoms of Beanie Babies. Looking at the tush tag is another good method for determining the approximate age of your Beanie. However, most collectors have been more interested in the hang tag generations when deciding how much to pay for a Beanie on the secondary market.

VERSION 1: Printed in black ink, this tag listed the country in which the Beanie was made and its contents: polyester fiber and/or P.V.C. (polyvinyl chloride) pellets.

1ST

VERSION 2: The red heart "ty" logo made its first appearance in the version 2 tush tag, which was the first to be printed in red ink.

2ND

VERSION 3: The Beanie's name appeared for the first time on the tag beneath a smaller heart logo, while "The Beanie Babies Collection™" appeared above the heart.

VERSION 4: A small red star was added to the upper left-hand side of the "ty" heart logo on this tush tag. Initially, a clear sticker with a red star was placed over the logo. By late 1997, these tags began appearing with

3RD

a registration mark and trademark symbol to read: "The Beanie Babies® Collection™." Another tweaking changed "The Beanie Babies Collection™" to a trademarked name, and collectors began noticing that some Beanies had tush tags with "P.E.," indicating a change to polyethylene pellets.

4TH

TUSH TAG TRIVIA

Beanie Babies produced exclusively for Canada have a second tush tag sewn into their bodies next to the U.S. tush tag. Printed in black ink in English and French, the Canadian tush tags are larger than their U.S. counterparts.

BEANIE BABIES® TOP TEN

*T*his section highlights the ten most valuable *Beanie Babies as determined by their secondary market value. Since the Beanie market is always up to something new (or for that matter, seemingly always on the rise), these Beanies have seen tremendous increases in the past few months. While this elite group is sure to make Beanie lovers' hearts beat a little faster, note that many of these crown jewels are variations or have hard-to-find early hang tags. Listed in parenthesis after the name is the generation hang tag that the price refers to. So, whether you're in the market or not, enjoy the following top of the charts because, as every collector knows, you just can't guess who may be next!*

#1 PEANUT™ (Dark blue, ③ – 3rd Generation) – $5,800

While it's been estimated that there were about 2,000 royal blue elephants shipped before production was stopped, we'll never really know for sure. Once the production error was noticed, Ty replaced the darker "Peanut" with a lighter version.

#2 BROWNIE™ (① – 1st Generation) – $4,600

One of the "Original Nine" Beanies, "Brownie" achieved notoriety when his name changed to "Cubbie" shortly after production started.

#3 NANA™ (③ – 3rd Generation) – $4,500

Like "Brownie," "Nana" received a name change soon after he was introduced. This Beanie now goes by the name of "Bongo" and is sure to keep creating "monkey business," as he has been known to sport both a brown and tan tail.

#4 DERBY™ (Fine mane, ③ – 3rd Generation) – $4,000

The first version of "Derby" was around briefly in 1995 and has collectors all over trying to distinguish between a fine or coarse mane. A "Derby" with a fine mane has more strands of thin yarn on its neck, while one with a coarse mane has fewer strands of thicker string.

#5 TEDDY™ (brown, old face, 🐾 – 1st Generation) – $3,600

Originally released with eyes spaced far apart and a pointy snout, this "old face" teddy was a hit with both Beanie and bear collectors everywhere. Only issued for about seven months, "Teddy" was soon given a "new face."

#6 CHILLY™ (🐾 – 1st Generation) – $2,800

Available for just over a year, "Chilly" is a hard-to-find Beanie. Adding to the difficulty is keeping the polar bear's pure white coat in mint condition; finding anyone who could keep their hands off this cuddly creature is next to impossible.

#7 HUMPHREY™ (🐾 – 1st Generation) – $2,750

Another Beanie available for just one year, "Humphrey" was not a big seller when he was first introduced. Now "Humphrey" is playing "hard-to-get" with all those collectors who ignored him when he was sitting on store shelves for $5.

#8 SLITHER™ (🐾 – 1st Generation) – $2,600

Issued in 1994, "Slither" was the first snake produced by Ty Inc. Since he, too, was available for just one year, he's been, well, slippery as a snake for even the most adept Beanie Babies hunters.

#9 PEKING™ (🐾 – 1st Generation) – $2,550

"Peking" was one of only four bears designed to lie flat on his stomach, which adds to the unique appeal of this exotic bear. "Peking" was produced for about one year before his 1996 retirement.

#10 QUACKERS™ (without wings, 🐾 – 1st Generation) – $2,500

While his winged counterpart was recently retired, "Quackers" without wings flew the coop long ago. It is believed that very few of the original "Quackers" were produced, with estimates being made at around 1,000.

HOW TO USE YOUR VALUE GUIDE

*I*t's easy to determine the current value of your Beanie Babies collection:

1. For each Beanie Babies plush animal you own, check off the "Got It!" box and write down the price paid and date purchased in the space provided. If only an estimated issue or retirement date is available, it is marked as "Est." Note: some poems for the May 1998 releases were unconfirmed or unavailable at press time.

TY TAG KEY

 ⑤ – 5th Generation

 ④ – 4th Generation

 ③ – 3rd Generation

 ② – 2nd Generation

 ① – 1st Generation

2. To determine the market value of your Beanie, first identify which hang tag is attached. To find out which generation tag your Beanie has, consult the chart to the left (for more details see pages 15-16). The market value for each generation tag is listed next to the appropriate symbol. For current Beanies with a 5th generation tag, fill in the current market value, which is usually the price you paid.

3. Add the "Market Value" of each Beanie you own and write the sum in the "Value Totals" box on each page. Be sure to use a pencil so you can make changes as your collection grows.

4. On page 104, write in your totals from each Value Guide page, then add the sums together to get the "Grand Total" of your Beanie collection!

Some current Beanie Babies with the 5th generation tag are relatively easy to find at the original retail price of $5-$7. Newly-released Beanies are often sold for a "higher than retail" price at first, which levels off a bit once the supply becomes more plentiful. Other hard to find current Beanies might sell for as much as $25-$40. Some Beanies are nearly impossible to find and can be sold for hundreds of dollars while still current.

In the Value Guide section all current Beanies are labeled according to the "degree of difficulty" in finding them at the original retail price. Happy hunting!

Just Released
Easy To Find
Moderate To Find
Hard To Find
Very Hard To Find
Impossible To Find

1997 Teddy™

①

Bear • #4200
Birthdate: December 25, 1996
Issued: October 1, 1997
Retired: December 31, 1997

Original Retail Price: $5-$7
○ Got it! • Paid: $_____
Date Purchased: _____

Market Value:
④–$60

Beanie Babies are special no doubt
All filled with love – inside and out
Wishes for fun times filled with joy
Ty's holiday teddy is a magical toy!

Ally™

②

Alligator • #4032
Birthdate: March 14, 1994
Issued: June 25, 1994
Retired: October 1, 1997

Original Retail Price: $5-$7
○ Got it! • Paid: $_____
Date Purchased: _____

Market Value:
④–$65 ③–$115 ②–$180
①–$300

When Ally gets out of classes
He wears a hat and dark glasses
He plays bass in a street band
He's the coolest gator in the land!

NEW!

Ants™

Anteater • #4195
Birthdate: November 7, 1997
Issued: May 30, 1998
Current – Just Released

Original Retail Price: $5-$7
○ Got it! • Paid: $_____
Date Purchased: _____

Market Value:
⑤-$_____

Most anteaters love to eat bugs
But this little fellow gives big hugs
He'd rather dine on apple pie
Than eat an ant or harm a fly!

Baldy™

Eagle • #4074
Birthdate: February 17, 1996
Issued: May 11, 1997
Retired: May 1, 1998

Original Retail Price: $5-$7
○ Got it! • Paid: $_____
Date Purchased: _____

Market Value:
⑤-$20 ④-$30

Hair on his head is quite scant
We suggest Baldy get a transplant
Watching over the land of the free
Hair in his eyes would make it hard to see!

Value
Totals _____

COLLECTOR'S
VALUE GUIDE™

Batty™

Bat • #4035
Birthdate: October 29, 1996
Issued: October 1, 1997
Current – Moderate To Find

Original Retail Price: $5-$7
○ Got it! • Paid: $_____
Date Purchased: _____

Market Value:
🖤5–$_____ 🖤4–$35

Bats may make some people jitter
Please don't be scared of this critter
If you're lonely or have nothing to do
This Beanie Baby would love to hug you!

Bernie™

St. Bernard • #4109
Birthdate: October 3, 1996
Issued: January 1, 1997
Current – Easy To Find

Original Retail Price: $5-$7
○ Got it! • Paid: $_____
Date Purchased: _____

Market Value:
🖤5–$_____ 🖤4–$10

This little dog can't wait to grow
To rescue people lost in the snow
Don't let him out – keep him on your shelf
He doesn't know how to rescue himself!

COLLECTOR'S
VALUE GUIDE™

Value
Totals _____

(7)

Bessie™
Cow • #4009
Birthdate: June 27, 1995
Issued: June 3, 1995
Retired: October 1, 1997

Original Retail Price: $5-$7
○ Got it! • Paid: $_____
Date Purchased: _____

Market Value:
❹–$75 ❸–$125

Bessie the cow likes to dance and sing
Because music is her favorite thing
Every night when you are counting sheep
She'll sing you a song to help you sleep!

(8)

Blackie™
Bear • #4011
Birthdate: July 15, 1994
Issued: June 25, 1994
Current – Easy To Find

Original Retail Price: $5-$7
○ Got it! • Paid: $_____
Date Purchased: _____

Market Value:
❺–$_____ ❹–$12 ❸–$70
❷–$150 ❶–$250

Living in a national park
He only played after dark
Then he met his friend Cubbie
Now they play when it's sunny!

Value
Totals _____

COLLECTOR'S
VALUE GUIDE™

Blizzard™

(9)

Tiger • #4163
Birthdate: December 12, 1996
Issued: May 11, 1997
Retired: May 1, 1998

Original Retail Price: $5-$7
○ Got it! • Paid: $_____
Date Purchased: _____

Market Value:
5-$25 **4**-$35

In the mountains, where it's snowy and cold
Lives a beautiful tiger, I've been told
Black and white, she's hard to compare
Of all the tigers, she is most rare!

Bones™

(10)

Dog • #4001
Birthdate: January 18, 1994
Issued: June 25, 1994
Retired: May 1, 1998

Original Retail Price: $5-$7
○ Got it! • Paid: $_____
Date Purchased: _____

Market Value:
5-$18 **4**-$25 **3**-$65
2-$140 **1**-$235

Bones is a dog that loves to chew
Chairs and tables and a smelly old shoe
"You're so destructive" all would shout
But that all stopped, when his teeth
Fell out!

COLLECTOR'S
VALUE GUIDE™

Value
Totals _____

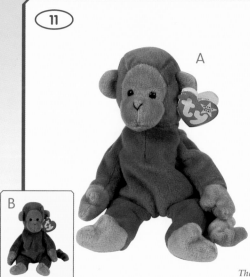

(11)

A

B

Bongo™
(name changed from "Nana" in 1995)
Monkey • #4067
Birthdate: August 17, 1995
Issued: June 3, 1995
Current – Moderate To Find

Original Retail Price: $5-$7
○ Got it! • Paid: $_____
Date Purchased: _____

Market Value:
A. Tan tail (June 95–Current)
5–$_____   **4**–$15   **3**–$105

B. Brown tail (Feb. 96–June 96)
4–$40   **3**–$110

Bongo the monkey lives in a tree
The happiest monkey you'll ever see
In his spare time he plays the guitar
One of these days he will be a big star!

(12)

Britannia™
(exclusive to Great Britain)
Bear • #4601
Birthdate: December 15, 1997
Issued: December 31, 1997
Current – Impossible To Find

Original Retail Price: $5-$7
○ Got it! • Paid: $_____
Date Purchased: _____

Market Value:
5–$_____

Britannia the bear will sail the sea
So she can be with you and me
She's always sure to catch the tide
And wear the Union Flag with pride

Value
Totals _____

COLLECTOR'S
VALUE GUIDE™

Bronty™

13

Brontosaurus • #4085
Birthdate: N/A
Issued: June 3, 1995
Retired: June 15, 1996

Original Retail Price: $5-$7
○ Got it! • Paid: $_____
Date Purchased: _____

Market Value:
③–$1,150

No Poem

_____
_____
_____

Brownie™

14

9
ORIGINAL
NINE

(name changed to "Cubbie" in 1994)
Bear • #4010
Birthdate: N/A
Issued: January 8, 1994
Out Of Production 1994

Original Retail Price: $5-$7
○ Got it! • Paid: $_____
Date Purchased: _____

Market Value:
①–$4,600

No Poem
_____
_____
_____

COLLECTOR'S
VALUE GUIDE™

Value
Totals _____

15

Bruno™
Dog • #4183
Birthdate: September 9, 1997
Issued: December 31, 1997
Current – Easy To Find

Original Retail Price: $5-$7
◯ Got it! • Paid: $_____
Date Purchased: _____

Market Value:
5–$_____

Bruno the dog thinks he's a brute
But all the other Beanies think he's cute
He growls at his tail and runs in a ring
And everyone says, "Oh, how darling!"

16

Bubbles™
Fish • #4078
Birthdate: July 2, 1995
Issued: June 3, 1995
Retired: May 11, 1997

Original Retail Price: $5-$7
◯ Got it! • Paid: $_____
Date Purchased: _____

Market Value:
4–$185 **3**–$260

All day long Bubbles likes to swim
She never gets tired of flapping her fins
Bubbles lived in a sea of blue
Now she is ready to come home with you!

Value
Totals _____

COLLECTOR'S
VALUE GUIDE™

Bucky™

(17)

Beaver • #4016
Birthdate: June 8, 1995
Issued: January 7, 1996
Retired: December 31, 1997

Original Retail Price: $5-$7
○ Got it! • Paid: $_____
Date Purchased: _____

Market Value:
4–$45 **3**–$110

*Bucky's teeth are as shiny as can be
Often used for cutting trees
He hides in his dam night and day
Maybe for you he will come out and play!*

Bumble™

(18)

Bee • #4045
Birthdate: October 16, 1995
Issued: June 3, 1995
Retired: June 15, 1996

Original Retail Price: $5-$7
○ Got it! • Paid: $_____
Date Purchased: _____

Market Value:
4–$750 **3**–$675

*Bumble the bee will not sting you
It is only love that this bee will bring you
So don't be afraid to give this bee a hug
Because Bumble the bee is a love-bug.*

COLLECTOR'S
VALUE GUIDE™

Value
Totals _____

19

Caw™
Crow • #4071
Birthdate: N/A
Issued: June 3, 1995
Retired: June 15, 1996

Original Retail Price: $5-$7
○ Got it! • Paid: $_____
Date Purchased: _____

Market Value:
❸–$775

No Poem
_____
_____
_____

20

Chilly™
Polar Bear • #4012
Birthdate: N/A
Issued: June 25, 1994
Retired: January 7, 1996

Original Retail Price: $5-$7
○ Got it! • Paid: $_____
Date Purchased: _____

Market Value:
❸–$2,500   ❷–$2,600
❶–$2,800

No Poem
_____
_____
_____

Value
Totals _____

COLLECTOR'S
VALUE GUIDE™

Chip™

Cat • #4121
Birthdate: January 26, 1996
Issued: May 11, 1997
Current – Moderate To Find

Original Retail Price: $5-$7
○ Got it! • Paid: $_____
Date Purchased: _____

Market Value:
5-$_____   *4*-$18

Black and gold, brown and white
The shades of her coat are quite a sight
At mixing her colors she was a master
On anyone else it would be a disaster!

Chocolate™

9
ORIGINAL
NINE

Moose • #4015
Birthdate: April 27, 1993
Issued: January 8, 1994
Current – Easy To Find

Original Retail Price: $5-$7
○ Got it! • Paid: $_____
Date Purchased: _____

Market Value:
5-$_____   *4*-$12   *3*-$75
2-$175   *1*-$275

Licorice, gum and peppermint candy
This moose always has these handy
There is one more thing he likes to eat
Can you guess his favorite sweet?

COLLECTOR'S
VALUE GUIDE™

Value
Totals _____

(23) Chops™

Lamb • #4019
Birthdate: May 3, 1996
Issued: January 7, 1996
Retired: January 1, 1997

Original Retail Price: $5-$7
○ Got it! • Paid: $_____
Date Purchased: _____

Market Value:
❹–$215 ❸–$280

Chops is a little lamb
This lamb you'll surely know
Because every path that you may take
This lamb is sure to go!

(24) Claude™

Crab • #4083
Birthdate: September 3, 1996
Issued: May 11, 1997
Current – Moderate To Find

Original Retail Price: $5-$7
○ Got it! • Paid: $_____
Date Purchased: _____

Market Value:
❺–$_____ ❹–$18

Claude the crab paints by the sea
A famous artist he hopes to be
But the tide came in and his paints fell
Now his art is on his shell!

Value
Totals _____

COLLECTOR'S
VALUE GUIDE™

Clubby™

(exclusive to Beanie Babies
Official Club members)
Bear • N/A
Birthdate: N/A
Issued: May 1, 1998
Current – Just Released

NEW!

Original Retail Price: $5.99
◯ Got it! • Paid: $_____
Date Purchased: _____

Market Value:
⑤–$_____

EXCLUSIVE FOR
BEANIE BABIES OFFICIAL
CLUB MEMBERS ONLY!

Poem Unavailable
_____
_____
_____

Congo™

Gorilla • #4160
Birthdate: November 9, 1996
Issued: June 15, 1996
Current – Easy To Find

Original Retail Price: $5-$7
◯ Got it! • Paid: $_____
Date Purchased: _____

Market Value:
⑤–$_____   ④–$12

Black as the night and fierce is he
On the ground or in a tree
Strong and mighty as the Congo
He's related to our Bongo!

COLLECTOR'S
VALUE GUIDE™

Value
Totals _____

(27)

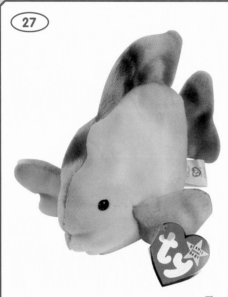

Coral™
Fish • #4079
Birthdate: March 2, 1995
Issued: June 3, 1995
Retired: January 1, 1997

Original Retail Price: $5-$7
○ Got it! • Paid: $_____
Date Purchased: _____

Market Value:
4-$230 **3**-$325

Coral is beautiful, as you know
Made of colors in the rainbow
Whether it's pink, yellow or blue
These colors were chosen just for you!

(28)

Crunch™
Shark • #4130
Birthdate: January 13, 1996
Issued: January 1, 1997
Current – Easy To Find

Original Retail Price: $5-$7
○ Got it! • Paid: $_____
Date Purchased: _____

Market Value:
5-$_____   **4**-$10

What's for breakfast? What's for lunch?
Yum! Delicious! Munch, munch, munch!
He's eating everything by the bunch
That's the reason we named him Crunch!

Value
Totals _____

COLLECTOR'S
VALUE GUIDE™

Cubbie™

(name changed from "Brownie" in 1994)
Bear • #4010
Birthdate: November 14, 1993
Issued: January 8, 1994
Retired: December 31, 1997

Original Retail Price: $5-$7
○ Got it! • Paid: $_____
Date Purchased: _____

Market Value:
④–$35 ③–$110 ②–$200
①–$350

29

9
ORIGINAL
NINE

*Cubbie used to eat crackers and honey
And what happened to him was funny
He was stung by fourteen bees
Now Cubbie eats broccoli and cheese!*

Curly™

Bear • #4052
Birthdate: April 12, 1996
Issued: June 15, 1996
Current – Hard To Find

Original Retail Price: $5-$7
○ Got it! • Paid: $_____
Date Purchased: _____

Market Value:
⑤–$_____ ④–$25

30

*A bear so cute with hair that's Curly
You will love and want him surely
To this bear always be true
He will be a friend to you!*

COLLECTOR'S
VALUE GUIDE™

Value
Totals _____

31

Daisy™
Cow • #4006
Birthdate: May 10, 1994
Issued: June 25, 1994
Current – Easy To Find

Original Retail Price: $5-$7
◯ Got it! • Paid: $_____
Date Purchased: _____

Market Value:
5-$_____ **4**-$12 **3**-$80
2-$195 **1**-$285

Daisy drinks milk each night
So her coat is shiny and bright
Milk is good for your hair and skin
What a way for your day to begin!

32

Derby™
Horse • #4008
Birthdate: September 16, 1995
Issued: June 3, 1995
Current – Moderate To Find

Original Retail Price: $5-$7
◯ Got it! • Paid: $_____
Date Purchased: _____

Market Value:
A. Star (Dec. 97–current)
5-$_____

B. Coarse mane (Est. Late 95–Dec. 97)
4-$30 **3**-$450

C. Fine mane (Est. June 95–
Late 95) **3**-$4,000

A

B

C

All the other horses used to tattle
Because Derby never wore his saddle
He left the stables, and the horses too
Just so Derby can be with you!

Value
Totals _____

COLLECTOR'S
VALUE GUIDE™

Digger™

(33)

Crab • #4027

Birthdate: August 23, 1995
Issued: June 25, 1994
Retired: May 11, 1997

Original Retail Price: $5-$7
○ Got it! • Paid: $_____
Date Purchased: _____

Market Value:
A. Red (June 95–May 97)
4–**$140** **3**–**$300**

B. Orange (June 94–June 95)
3–**$790** **2**–**$850** **1**–**$880**

A

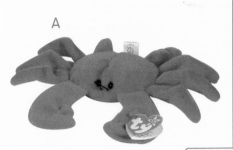

*Digging in the sand and walking sideways
That's how Digger spends her days
Hard on the outside but sweet deep inside
Basking in the sun and riding the tide!*

B

Doby™

(34)

Doberman • #4110

Birthdate: October 9, 1996
Issued: January 1, 1997
Current – Easy To Find

Original Retail Price: $5-$7
○ Got it! • Paid: $_____
Date Purchased: _____

Market Value:
5–**$_____** **4**–**$12**

*This dog is little but he has might
Keep him close when you sleep at night
He lays around with nothing to do
Until he sees it's time to protect you!*

COLLECTOR'S
VALUE GUIDE™

Value
Totals _____

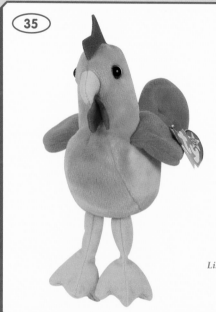

(35)

Doodle™
(name changed to "Strut" in 1997)
Rooster • #4171
Birthdate: March 8, 1996
Issued: May 11, 1997
Out Of Production 1997

Original Retail Price: $5-$7
○ Got it! • Paid: $_____
Date Purchased: _____

Market Value:
❹–$60

Listen closely to "cock-a-doodle-doo"
What's the rooster saying to you?
Hurry, wake up sleepy head
We have lots to do, get out of bed!

(36)

Dotty™
Dalmatian • #4100
Birthdate: October 17, 1996
Issued: May 11, 1997
Current – Easy To Find

Original Retail Price: $5-$7
○ Got it! • Paid: $_____
Date Purchased: _____

Market Value:
❺–$_____   ❹–$12

The Beanies all thought it was a big joke
While writing her tag, their ink pen broke
She got in the way, and got all spotty
So now the Beanies call her Dotty!

Value
Totals _____

COLLECTOR'S
VALUE GUIDE™

Early™

Robin • #4190
Birthdate: February 20, 1997
Issued: May 30, 1998
Current – Just Released

Original Retail Price: $5-$7
○ Got it! • Paid: $_____
Date Purchased: _____

Market Value:
⑤-$_____

37

NEW!

*Early is a red breasted robin
For worms he'll soon be bobbin'
Known as a sign of spring
This happy robin loves to sing!*

Ears™

Rabbit • #4018
Birthdate: April 18, 1995
Issued: January 7, 1996
Retired: May 1, 1998

Original Retail Price: $5-$7
○ Got it! • Paid: $_____
Date Purchased: _____

Market Value:
⑤-$18 ④-$27 ③-$80

38

*He's been eating carrots so long
Didn't understand what was wrong
Couldn't see the board during classes
Until the doctor gave him glasses!*

COLLECTOR'S
VALUE GUIDE™

Value
Totals _____

(39)

Echo™
Dolphin • #4180
Birthdate: December 21, 1996
Issued: May 11, 1997
Retired: May 1, 1998

Original Retail Price: $5-$7
◯ Got it! • Paid: $_____
Date Purchased: _____

Market Value:
⑤–$18   ④–$27

Echo the dolphin lives in the sea
Playing with her friends, like you and me
Through the waves she echoes the sound
"I'm so glad to have you around!"

(40)

Erin™
Bear • #4186
Birthdate: March 17, 1997
Issued: January 31, 1998
Current – Impossible To Find

Original Retail Price: $5-$7
◯ Got it! • Paid: $_____
Date Purchased: _____

Market Value:
⑤–$_____

Named after the beautiful Emerald Isle
This Beanie Baby will make you smile,
A bit of luck, a pot of gold,
Light up the faces, both young and old!

Value
Totals _____

COLLECTOR'S
VALUE GUIDE™

Fetch™

41

NEW!

Golden Retriever • #4189
Birthdate: February 4, 1997
Issued: May 30, 1998
Current – Just Released

Original Retail Price: $5-$7
○ Got it! • Paid: $_____
Date Purchased: _____

Market Value:
**$5**–$_____

Fetch is alert at the crack of dawn
Walking through dewdrops on the lawn
Always golden, loyal and true
This little puppy is the one for you!

Flash™

42

9
ORIGINAL NINE

Dolphin • #4021
Birthdate: May 13, 1993
Issued: January 8, 1994
Retired: May 11, 1997

Original Retail Price: $5-$7
○ Got it! • Paid: $_____
Date Purchased: _____

Market Value:
4–$150 **3**–$220 **2**–$295
1–$385

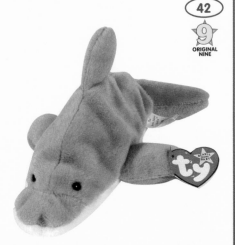

You know dolphins are a smart breed
Our friend Flash knows how to read
Splash the whale is the one who taught her
Although reading is difficult under the water!

COLLECTOR'S
VALUE GUIDE™

Value
Totals _____

Fleece™
Lamb • #4125
Birthdate: March 21, 1996
Issued: January 1, 1997
Current – Easy To Find

Original Retail Price: $5-$7
○ Got it! • Paid: $_____
Date Purchased: _____

Market Value:
⑤-$_____   ④-$15

Fleece would like to sing a lullaby
But please be patient, she's rather shy
When you sleep, keep her by your ear
Her song will leave you nothing to fear.

Flip™
Cat • #4012
Birthdate: February 28, 1995
Issued: January 7, 1996
Retired: October 1, 1997

Original Retail Price: $5-$7
○ Got it! • Paid: $_____
Date Purchased: _____

Market Value:
④-$45   ③-$125

Flip the cat is an acrobat
She loves playing on her mat
This cat flips with such grace and flair
She can somersault in mid air!

Value
Totals _____

COLLECTOR'S
VALUE GUIDE™

Floppity™

Bunny • #4118
Birthdate: May 28, 1996
Issued: January 1, 1997
Retired: May 1, 1998

Original Retail Price: $5-$7
○ Got it! • Paid: $_____
Date Purchased: _____

Market Value:
⑤–$23 ④–$32

Floppity hops from here to there
Searching for eggs without a care
Lavender coat from head to toe
All dressed up and nowhere to go!

Flutter™

Butterfly • #4043
Birthdate: N/A
Issued: June 3, 1995
Retired: June 15, 1996

Original Retail Price: $5-$7
○ Got it! • Paid: $_____
Date Purchased: _____

Market Value:
③–$1,150

No Poem
_____
_____
_____
_____

COLLECTOR'S
VALUE GUIDE™

Value
Totals _____

47

NEW!

Fortune™
Panda • #4196
Birthdate: December 6, 1997
Issued: May 30, 1998
Current – Just Released

Original Retail Price: $5-$7
○ Got it! • Paid: $_____
Date Purchased: _____

Market Value:
⑤–$_____

Nibbling on a bamboo tree
This little panda is hard to see
You're so lucky with this one you found
Only a few are still around!

48

Freckles™
Leopard • #4066
Birthdate: June 3, 1996 or
July 28, 1996
Issued: June 15, 1996
Current – Easy To Find

Original Retail Price: $5-$7
○ Got it! • Paid: $_____
Date Purchased: _____

Market Value:
⑤–$_____   ④–$12

From the trees he hunts prey
In the night and in the day
He's the king of camouflage
Look real close, he's no mirage!

Value
Totals _____

COLLECTOR'S
VALUE GUIDE™

Garcia™

Bear • #4051
Birthdate: August 1, 1995
Issued: January 7, 1996
Retired: May 11, 1997

Original Retail Price: $5-$7
○ Got it! • Paid: $_____
Date Purchased: _____

Market Value:
④–$225 **③**–$280

49

The Beanies use to follow him around
Because Garcia traveled from town to town
He's pretty popular as you can see
Some even say he's legendary!

Gigi•™

Poodle • #4191
Birthdate: March 7, 1997
Issued: May 30, 1998
Current – Just Released

Original Retail Price: $5-$7
○ Got it! • Paid: $_____
Date Purchased: _____

Market Value:
⑤–$_____

50

NEW!

Poem Unavailable
_____
_____
_____
_____

COLLECTOR'S
VALUE GUIDE™

Value
Totals _____

Glory™

Bear • #4188
Birthdate: July 4, 1997
Issued: May 30, 1998
Current – Just Released

Original Retail Price: $5-$7
○ Got it! • Paid: $_____
Date Purchased: _____

Market Value:
⑤-$_____

*Oh say can you see
Glory's proud of her country
Born on Independence Day
This bear lives in the USA!*

51 NEW!

52

Gobbles™

Turkey • #4034
Birthdate: November 27, 1996
Issued: October 1, 1997
Current – Moderate To Find

Original Retail Price: $5-$7
○ Got it! • Paid: $_____
Date Purchased: _____

Market Value:
⑤-$_____ ④-$40

*Gobbles the turkey loves to eat
Once a year she has a feast
I have a secret I'd like to divulge
If she eats too much her tummy will bulge!*

Value
Totals _____

Goldie™

Goldfish • #4023
Birthdate: November 14, 1994
Issued: June 25, 1994
Retired: December 31, 1997

Original Retail Price: $5-$7
○ Got it! • Paid: $_____
Date Purchased: _____

Market Value:
④–$50 **③**–$120 **②**–$235
①–$325

She's got rhythm, she's got soul
What more to like in a fish bowl?
Through sound waves Goldie swam
Because this goldfish likes to jam!

Gracie™

Swan • #4126
Birthdate: June 17, 1996
Issued: January 1, 1997
Retired: May 1, 1998

Original Retail Price: $5-$7
○ Got it! • Paid: $_____
Date Purchased: _____

Market Value:
⑤–$18 **④**–$27

As a duckling, she was confused,
Birds on the lake were quite amused.
Poking fun until she would cry,
Now the most beautiful swan at Ty!

COLLECTOR'S
VALUE GUIDE™

Value
Totals _____

55

Grunt™
Razorback • #4092
Birthdate: July 19, 1995
Issued: January 7, 1996
Retired: May 11, 1997

Original Retail Price: $5-$7
○ Got it! • Paid: $_____
Date Purchased: _____

Market Value:
4–$230 **3**–$290

Some Beanies think Grunt is tough
No surprise, he's scary enough
But if you take him home you'll see
Grunt is the sweetest Beanie Baby!

56

Happy™
Hippo • #4061
Birthdate: February 25, 1994
Issued: June 25, 1994
Retired: May 1, 1998

Original Retail Price: $5-$7
○ Got it! • Paid: $_____
Date Purchased: _____

Market Value:
A. Lavender (June 95–May 98)
5–$20 **4**–$29 **3**–$285

B. Gray (June 94–June 95)
3–$825 **2**–$850 **1**–$890

A

B

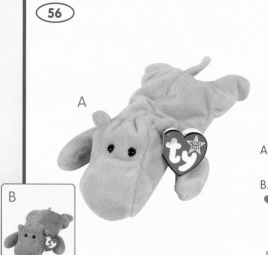

Happy the Hippo loves to wade
In the river and in the shade
When Happy shoots water out of his snout
You know he's happy without a doubt!

Value
Totals _____

COLLECTOR'S
VALUE GUIDE™

Hippity™

Bunny • #4119
Birthdate: June 1, 1996
Issued: January 1, 1997
Retired: May 1, 1998

Original Retail Price: $5-$7
◯ Got it! • Paid: $_____
Date Purchased: _____

Market Value:
🟡–$23 🔵–$32

Hippity is a cute little bunny
Dressed in green, he looks quite funny
Twitching his nose in the air
Sniffing a flower here and there!

Hissy™

Snake • #4185
Birthdate: April 4, 1997
Issued: December 31, 1997
Current – Moderate To Find

Original Retail Price: $5-$7
◯ Got it! • Paid: $_____
Date Purchased: _____

Market Value:
🟡–$_____

Curled and coiled and ready to play
He waits for you patiently every day
He'll keep his best friend, but not his skin
And stay with you through thick and thin.

COLLECTOR'S
VALUE GUIDE™

Value
Totals _____

59

Hoot™
Owl • #4073
Birthdate: August 9, 1995
Issued: January 7, 1996
Retired: October 1, 1997

Original Retail Price: $5-$7
○ Got it! • Paid: $_____
Date Purchased: _____

Market Value:
4–$50 **3**–$130

Late to bed, late to rise
Nevertheless, Hoot's quite wise
Studies by candlelight, nothing new
Like a president, do you know Whooo?

60

Hoppity™
Bunny • #4117
Birthdate: April 3, 1996
Issued: January 1, 1997
Retired: May 1, 1998

Original Retail Price: $5-$7
○ Got it! • Paid: $_____
Date Purchased: _____

Market Value:
5–$23 **4**–$32

Hopscotch is what she likes to play
If you don't join in, she'll hop away
So play a game if you have the time,
She likes to play, rain or shine!

Value
Totals _____

COLLECTOR'S
VALUE GUIDE™

Humphrey™

Camel • #4060
Birthdate: N/A
Issued: June 25, 1994
Retired: June 15, 1995

Original Retail Price: $5-$7
○ Got it! • Paid: $_____
Date Purchased: _____

Market Value:
❸–$2,500 ❷–$2,650
❶–$2,750

No Poem

_____
_____
_____

Iggy™

Iguana • #4038
Birthdate: August 12, 1997
Issued: December 31, 1997
Current – Hard To Find

Original Retail Price: $5-$7
○ Got it! • Paid: $_____
Date Purchased: _____

Market Value:
❺–$_____

Sitting on a rock, basking in the sun
Is this iguana's idea of fun
Towel and glasses, book and beach chair
His life is so perfect without a care!

COLLECTOR'S
VALUE GUIDE™

Value
Totals _____

63

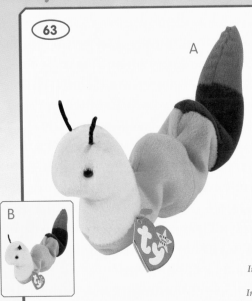

A

Inch™
Inchworm • #4044
Birthdate: September 3, 1995
Issued: June 3, 1995
Retired: May 1, 1998

Original Retail Price: $5-$7
○ Got it! • Paid: $_____
Date Purchased: _____

Market Value:
A. Yarn antennas
(Est. Mid 96–May 98)
5–$23 **4**–$35

B. Felt antennas
(Est. June 95–Mid 96)
4–$190 **3**–$215

B

Inch the worm is a friend of mine
He goes so slow all the time
Inching around from here to there
Traveling the world without a care!

64

A

Inky™
Octopus • #4028
Birthdate: November 29, 1994
Issued: June 25, 1994
Retired: May 1, 1998

Original Retail Price: $5-$7
○ Got it! • Paid: $_____
Date Purchased: _____

Market Value:
A. Pink (June 95–May 98)
5–$35 **4**–$45 **3**–$330

B. Tan with mouth (Sept. 94–June 95)
3–$775 **2**–$790

C. Tan without mouth (June 94–
Sept. 94) **2**–$825 **1**–$850

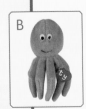
B

C

Inky's head is big and round
As he swims he makes no sound
If you need a hand, don't hesitate
Inky can help because he has eight!

Value
Totals _____

Jabber™

Parrot • #4197
Birthdate: October 10, 1997
Issued: May 30, 1998
Current – Just Released

Original Retail Price: $5-$7
○ Got it! • Paid: $_____
Date Purchased: _____

Market Value:
$5-$_____

65

NEW!

Poem Unavailable
_____
_____
_____

Jake™

Mallard Duck • #4199
Birthdate: April 16, 1997
Issued: May 30, 1998
Current – Just Released

Original Retail Price: $5-$7
○ Got it! • Paid: $_____
Date Purchased: _____

Market Value:
$5-$_____

66

NEW!

Jake the drake likes to splash in a puddle
Take him home and give him a cuddle
Quack, Quack, Quack, he will say
He's so glad you're here to play!

COLLECTOR'S
VALUE GUIDE™

Value
Totals _____

67

Jolly™
Walrus • #4082
Birthdate: December 2, 1996
Issued: May 11, 1997
Retired: May 1, 1998

Original Retail Price: $5-$7
○ Got it! • Paid: $_____
Date Purchased: _____

Market Value:
5–$25 **4**–$35

Jolly the walrus is not very serious
He laughs and laughs until he's delirious
He often reminds me of my dad
Always happy, never sad!

68

Kiwi™
Toucan • #4070
Birthdate: September 16, 1995
Issued: June 3, 1995
Retired: January 1, 1997

Original Retail Price: $5-$7
○ Got it! • Paid: $_____
Date Purchased: _____

Market Value:
4–$235 **3**–$300

Kiwi waits for the April showers
Watching a garden bloom with flowers
There trees grow with fruit that's sweet
I'm sure you'll guess his favorite treat!

Value
Totals _____

COLLECTOR'S
VALUE GUIDE™

Kuku™

Cockatoo • #4192
Birthdate: January 5, 1997
Issued: May 30, 1998
Current – Just Released

Original Retail Price: $5-$7
○ Got it! • Paid: $_____
Date Purchased: _____

Market Value:
5–$_____

This fancy bird loves to converse
He talks in poems, rhythms and verse
So take him home and give him some time
You'll be surprised how he can rhyme

Lefty™

70

Donkey • #4085
Birthdate: July 4, 1996
Issued: June 15, 1996
Retired: January 1, 1997

Original Retail Price: $5-$7
○ Got it! • Paid: $_____
Date Purchased: _____

Market Value:
4–$450

Donkeys to the left, elephants to the right
Often seems like a crazy sight
This whole game seems very funny
Until you realize they're spending
Your money!

COLLECTOR'S™
VALUE GUIDE

Value
Totals _____

71

ORIGINAL NINE

Legs™
Frog • #4020
Birthdate: April 25, 1993
Issued: January 8, 1994
Retired: October 1, 1997

Original Retail Price: $5-$7
○ Got it! • Paid: $_____
Date Purchased: _____

Market Value:
4–$35 **3**–$115 **2**–$225
1–$310

Legs lives in a hollow log
Legs likes to play leap frog
If you like to hang out at the lake
Legs will be the new friend you'll make!

72

Libearty™
Bear • #4057
Birthdate: Summer 1996
Issued: June 15, 1996
Retired: January 1, 1997

Original Retail Price: $5-$7
○ Got it! • Paid: $_____
Date Purchased: _____

Market Value:
4–$520

I am called libearty
I wear the flag for all to see
Hope and freedom is my way
That's why I wear flag USA

Value
Totals _____

COLLECTOR'S
VALUE GUIDE™

Lizzy™

Lizard • #4033
Birthdate: May 11, 1995
Issued: June 3, 1995
Retired: December 31, 1997

Original Retail Price: $5-$7
○ Got it! • Paid: $_____
Date Purchased: _____

Market Value:
A. Blue (Jan. 96–Dec. 97)
④–**$35** ③–**$340**

B. Tie-dye (June 95–Jan. 96)
③–**$1,100**

B

Lizzy loves Legs the frog
She hides with him under logs
Both of them search for flies
Underneath the clear blue skies!

Lucky™

Ladybug • #4040
Birthdate: May 1, 1995
Issued: June 25, 1994
Retired: May 1, 1998

Original Retail Price: $5-$7
○ Got it! • Paid: $_____
Date Purchased: _____

Market Value:
A. Approx. 11 printed spots (Feb.
96–May 98) ⑤–**$23** ④–**$35**

B. Approx. 21 printed spots
(Est. Mid 96–Late 96) ④–**$680**

C. Approx. 7 felt glued-on spots
(June 94–Feb. 96)
③–**$240** ②–**$330** ①–**$415**

A

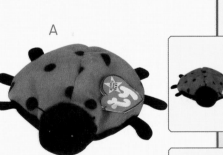

B

C

Lucky the lady bug loves the lotto
"Someone must win" that's her motto
But save your dimes and even a penny
Don't spend on the lotto and
You'll have many!

COLLECTOR'S
VALUE GUIDE™

Value
Totals _____

75

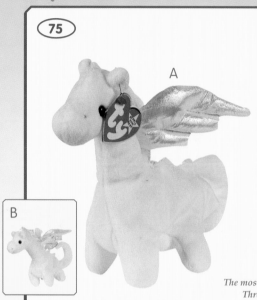

A

B

Magic™
Dragon • #4088
Birthdate: September 5, 1995
Issued: June 3, 1995
Retired: December 31, 1997

Original Retail Price: $5-$7
○ Got it! • Paid: $_____
Date Purchased: _____

Market Value:
A. Pale pink thread
(June 95–Dec. 97)
4–**$60** **3**–**$110**

B. Hot pink thread
(Est. Mid 96–Early 97)
4–**$85**

Magic the dragon lives in a dream
The most beautiful that you have ever seen
Through magic lands she likes to fly
Look up and watch her, way up high!

76

Manny™
Manatee • #4081
Birthdate: June 8, 1995
Issued: January 7, 1996
Retired: May 11, 1997

Original Retail Price: $5-$7
○ Got it! • Paid: $_____
Date Purchased: _____

Market Value:
4–**$205** **3**–**$275**

Manny is sometimes called a sea cow
She likes to twirl and likes to bow
Manny sure is glad you bought her
Because it's so lonely under water!

Value
Totals _____

COLLECTOR'S
VALUE GUIDE™

Maple™

(exclusive to Canada)
Bear • #4600
Birthdate: July 1, 1996
Issued: January 1, 1997
Current – Impossible To Find

A

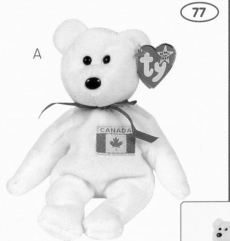

Original Retail Price: $5-$7
○ Got it! • Paid: $_____
Date Purchased: _____

Market Value:

A. "Maple" tush tag
(Est. Early 97–Current)
⑤-$_____ **④**-**$325**

B. "Pride" tush tag (Est. Jan. 97–
Early 97) **④**-**$700**

B

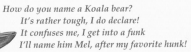
*Maple the bear likes to ski
With his friends, he plays hockey.
He loves his pancakes and eats every crumb
Can you guess which country he's from?*

Mel™

Koala • #4162
Birthdate: January 15, 1996
Issued: January 1, 1997
Current – Easy To Find

Original Retail Price: $5-$7
○ Got it! • Paid: $_____
Date Purchased: _____

Market Value:
⑤-$_____ **④**-**$12**

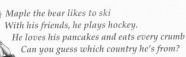
*How do you name a Koala bear?
It's rather tough, I do declare!
It confuses me, I get into a funk
I'll name him Mel, after my favorite hunk!*

COLLECTOR'S
VALUE GUIDE™

Value
Totals _____

(79)

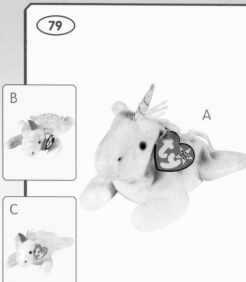

B

C

A

Mystic™
Unicorn • #4007
Birthdate: May 21, 1994
Issued: June 25, 1994
Current – Moderate To Find

Original Retail Price: $5-$7
○ Got it! • Paid: $_____
Date Purchased: _____

Market Value:
A. Iridescent horn (Oct. 97–Current)
⑤-$_____ ④-$35

B. Brown horn/coarse mane (Est. Late
95–Oct. 97) **④-$50 ③-$110**

C. Brown horn/fine mane
(Est. June 94–Late 95)
③-$285 ②-$355 ①-$430

*Once upon a time so far away
A unicorn was born one day in May
Keep Mystic with you, she's a prize
You'll see the magic in her blue eyes!*

(80)

Nana™
(name changed to "Bongo" in 1995)
Monkey • #4067
Birthdate: N/A
Issued: June 3, 1995
Out Of Production 1995

Original Retail Price: $5-$7
○ Got it! • Paid: $_____
Date Purchased: _____

Market Value:
③-$4,500

No Poem
_____
_____
_____
_____

Value
Totals _____

Nanook™

Husky • #4104
Birthdate: November 21, 1996
Issued: May 11, 1997
Current – Moderate To Find

Original Retail Price: $5-$7
○ Got it! • Paid: $_____
Date Purchased: _____

Market Value:
5-$_____ **4**-$20

Nanook is a dog that loves cold weather
To him a sled is light as a feather
Over the snow and through the slush
He runs at hearing the cry of "mush"!

Nip™

Cat • #4003
Birthdate: March 6, 1994
Issued: January 7, 1995
Retired: December 31, 1997

Original Retail Price: $5-$7
○ Got it! • Paid: $_____
Date Purchased: _____

Market Value:

A. White paws (March 96–Dec. 97)
   4-$40 **3**-$325

B. All gold (Jan. 96–March 96)
   3-$925

C. White face (Jan. 95–Jan. 96)
   3-$525 **2**-$560

A

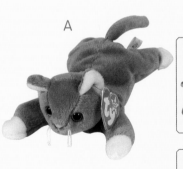

B

C

His name is Nipper, but we call him Nip
His best friend is a black cat named Zip
Nip likes to run in races for fun
He runs so fast he's always number one!

COLLECTOR'S
VALUE GUIDE™

Value
Totals _____

83

Nuts™
Squirrel • #4114
Birthdate: January 21, 1996
Issued: January 1, 1997
Current – Easy To Find

Original Retail Price: $5-$7
○ Got it! • Paid: $_____
Date Purchased: _____

Market Value:
⑤–$_____ ④–$15

With his bushy tail, he'll scamper up a tree
The most cheerful critter you'll ever see,
He's nuts about nuts, and he loves to chat
Have you ever seen a squirrel like that?

84

ORIGINAL
NINE

Patti™
Platypus • #4025
Birthdate: January 6, 1993
Issued: January 8, 1994
Retired: May 1, 1998

Original Retail Price: $5-$7
○ Got it! • Paid: $_____
Date Purchased: _____

Market Value:
A. Magenta (Feb. 95–May 98)
⑤–$28 ④–$35 ③–$310

B. Maroon (Jan. 94–Feb. 95)
③–$875 ②–$1,180 ①–$1,250

A

B

Ran into Patti one day while walking
Believe me she wouldn't stop talking
Listened and listened to her speak
That would explain her extra large beak!

Value
Totals _____

COLLECTOR'S
VALUE GUIDE™

Peace™

Bear • #4053
Birthdate: February 1, 1996
Issued: May 11, 1997
Current – Very Hard To Find

Original Retail Price: $5-$7
○ Got it! • Paid: $_____
Date Purchased: _____

Market Value:
⑤-$_____ ④-$55

All races, all colors, under the sun
Join hands together and have some fun
Dance to the music, rock and roll is the sound
Symbols of peace and love abound!

Peanut™

Elephant • #4062
Birthdate: January 25, 1995
Issued: June 3, 1995
Retired: May 1, 1998

Original Retail Price: $5-$7
○ Got it! • Paid: $_____
Date Purchased: _____

Market Value:
A. Light blue (Oct. 95–May 98)
⑤-$25 ④-$33 ③-$1,350

B. Dark blue (June 95–Oct. 95)
③-$5,800

A

B

Peanut the elephant walks on tip-toes
Quietly sneaking wherever she goes
She'll sneak up on you and a hug
You will get
Peanut is a friend you won't soon forget!

COLLECTOR'S
VALUE GUIDE™

Value
Totals _____

87

Peking™
Panda • #4013
Birthdate: N/A
Issued: June 25, 1994
Retired: January 7, 1996

Original Retail Price: $5-$7
○ Got it! • Paid: $_____
Date Purchased: _____

Market Value:
3–$2,300 **2**–$2,400
1–$2,550

No Poem

_____
_____
_____
_____

88

9
**ORIGINAL
NINE**

Pinchers™
Lobster • #4026
Birthdate: June 19, 1993
Issued: January 8, 1994
Retired: May 1, 1998

Original Retail Price: $5-$7
○ Got it! • Paid: $_____
Date Purchased: _____

Market Value:
5–$23 **4**–$30 **3**–$100
2–$195 **1**–$280

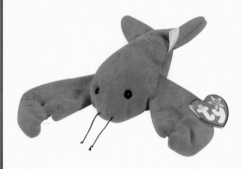

*This lobster loves to pinch
Eating his food inch by inch
Balancing carefully with his tail
Moving forward slow as a snail!*

Value
Totals _____

COLLECTOR'S
VALUE GUIDE™

Pinky™

Flamingo • #4072
Birthdate: February 13, 1995
Issued: June 3, 1995
Current – Moderate To Find

Original Retail Price: $5-$7
○ Got it! • Paid: $_____
Date Purchased: _____

Market Value:
⑤-$_____ ④-$18 ③-$105

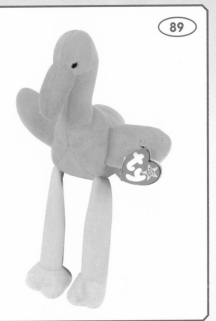

Pinky loves the everglades
From the hottest pink she's made
With floppy legs and big orange beak
She's the Beanie that you seek!

Pouch™

Kangaroo • #4161
Birthdate: November 6, 1996
Issued: January 1, 1997
Current – Moderate To Find

Original Retail Price: $5-$7
○ Got it! • Paid: $_____
Date Purchased: _____

Market Value:
⑤-$_____ ④-$16

My little pouch is handy I've found
It helps me carry my baby around
I hop up and down without any fear
Knowing my baby is safe and near.

COLLECTOR'S
VALUE GUIDE™

Value
Totals _____

(91)

Pounce™
Cat • #4122
Birthdate: August 28, 1997
Issued: December 31, 1997
Current – Moderate To Find

Original Retail Price: $5-$7
○ Got it! • Paid: **$_____**
Date Purchased: _____

Market Value:
⑤– **$_____**

Sneaking and slinking down the hall
To pounce upon a fluffy yarn ball
Under the tables, around the chairs
Through the rooms and down the stairs!

(92)

Prance™
Cat • #4123
Birthdate: November 20, 1997
Issued: December 31, 1997
Current – Moderate To Find

Original Retail Price: $5-$7
○ Got it! • Paid: **$_____**
Date Purchased: _____

Market Value:
⑤– **$_____**

She darts around and swats the air
Then looks confused when nothing's there
Pick her up and pet her soft fur
Listen closely, and you'll hear her purr!

Value
Totals _____

COLLECTOR'S
VALUE GUIDE™

Princess™

(93)

Bear • #4300
Birthdate: N/A
Issued: October 29, 1997
Current – Impossible To Find

Original Retail Price: $5-$7
◯ Got it! • Paid: $_____
Date Purchased: _____

Market Value:
⑤-$_____   ④-$225

Like an angel, she came from heaven above
She shared her compassion, her pain, her love
She only stayed with us long enough to teach
The world to share, to give, to reach.

Puffer™

(94)

Puffin • #4181
Birthdate: November 3, 1997
Issued: December 31, 1997
Current – Easy To Find

Original Retail Price: $5-$7
◯ Got it! • Paid: $_____
Date Purchased: _____

Market Value:
⑤-$_____

What in the world does a puffin do?
We're sure that you would like to know too
We asked Puffer how she spends her days
Before she answered, she flew away!

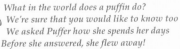

COLLECTOR'S
VALUE GUIDE™

Value
Totals _____

95

Pugsly™
Pug Dog • #4106
Birthdate: May 2, 1996
Issued: May 11, 1997
Current – Moderate To Find

Original Retail Price: $5-$7
○ Got it! • Paid: $_____
Date Purchased: _____

Market Value:
❺-$_____   ❹-$15

Pugsly is picky about what he will wear
Never a spot, a stain or a tear
Image is something of which he'll gloat
Until he noticed his wrinkled coat!

96

Quackers™
Duck • #4024
Birthdate: April 19, 1994
Issued: June 25, 1994
Retired: May 1, 1998

Original Retail Price: $5-$7
○ Got it! • Paid: $_____
Date Purchased: _____

Market Value:
A. With wings (Jan. 95–May 98)
❺-$23   ❹-$30   ❸-$110
❷-$500
B. Without wings (June 94–Jan. 95)
❷-$2,400   ❶-$2,500

A

B

There is a duck by the name of Quackers
Every night he eats animal crackers
He swims in a lake that's clear and blue
But he'll come to the shore to be with you!

Value
Totals _____

Radar™

Bat • #4091
Birthdate: October 30, 1995
Issued: September 1, 1995
Retired: May 11, 1997

Original Retail Price: $5-$7
○ Got it! • Paid: $_____
Date Purchased: _____

Market Value:
❹-$210 ❸-$275

Radar the bat flies late at night
He can soar to an amazing height
If you see something as high as a star
Take a good look, it might be Radar!

Rainbow™

Chameleon • #4037
Birthdate: October 14, 1997
Issued: December 31, 1997
Current – Hard To Find

Original Retail Price: $5-$7
○ Got it! • Paid: $_____
Date Purchased: _____

Market Value:
❺-$_____

Red, green, blue and yellow
This chameleon is a colorful fellow.
A blend of colors, his own unique hue
Rainbow was made especially for you!

COLLECTOR'S
VALUE GUIDE™

Value
Totals _____

(99)

Rex™
Tyrannosaurus • #4086
Birthdate: N/A
Issued: June 3, 1995
Retired: June 15, 1996

Original Retail Price: $5-$7
○ Got it! • Paid: $_____
Date Purchased: _____

Market Value:
❸–$1,000

No Poem

_____
_____
_____

(100)

Righty™
Elephant • #4086
Birthdate: July 4, 1996
Issued: June 15, 1996
Retired: January 1, 1997

Original Retail Price: $5-$7
○ Got it! • Paid: $_____
Date Purchased: _____

Market Value:
❹–$450

Donkeys to the left, elephants to the right
Often seems like a crazy sight
This whole game seems very funny
Until you realize they're spending
Your money!

Value
Totals _____

Ringo™

Raccoon • #4014
Birthdate: July 14, 1995
Issued: January 7, 1996
Current – Easy To Find

Original Retail Price: $5-$7
○ Got it! • Paid: $_____
Date Purchased: _____

Market Value:
⑤-$_____ ④-$16 ③-$100

(101)

Ringo hides behind his mask
He will come out, if you should ask
He loves to chitter. He loves to chatter
Just about anything, it doesn't matter!

Roary™

Lion • #4069
Birthdate: February 20, 1996
Issued: May 11, 1997
Current – Easy To Find

Original Retail Price: $5-$7
○ Got it! • Paid: $_____
Date Purchased: _____

Market Value:
⑤-$_____ ④-$16

(102)

Deep in the jungle they crowned him king
But being brave is not his thing
A cowardly lion some may say
He hears his roar and runs away!

COLLECTOR'S
VALUE GUIDE™

Value
Totals _____

103

NEW!

Rocket™
Blue Jay • #4202
Birthdate: March 12, 1997
Issued: May 30, 1998
Current – Just Released

Original Retail Price: $5-$7
◯ Got it! • Paid: $_____
Date Purchased: _____

Market Value:
⑤-$_____

Poem Unavailable

_____
_____
_____

104

Rover™
Dog • #4101
Birthdate: May 30, 1996
Issued: June 15, 1996
Retired: May 1, 1998

Original Retail Price: $5-$7
◯ Got it! • Paid: $_____
Date Purchased: _____

Market Value:
⑤-$20 ④-$28

This dog is red and his name is Rover
If you call him he is sure to come over
He barks and plays with all his might
But worry not, he won't bite!

Value
Totals _____

Scoop™

Pelican • #4107
Birthdate: July 1, 1996
Issued: June 15, 1996
Current – Moderate To Find

Original Retail Price: $5-$7
◯ Got it! • Paid: $_____
Date Purchased: _____

Market Value:
⑤-$_____ ④-$17

All day long he scoops up fish
To fill his bill, is his wish
Diving fast and diving low
Hoping those fish are very slow!

Scottie™

Scottish Terrier • #4102
Birthdate: June 3, 1996 or
June 15, 1996
Issued: June 15, 1996
Retired: May 1, 1998

Original Retail Price: $5-$7
◯ Got it! • Paid: $_____
Date Purchased: _____

Market Value:
⑤-$23 ④-$30

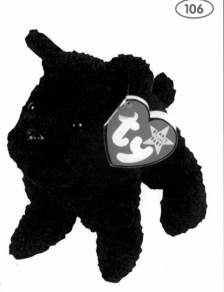

Scottie is a friendly sort
Even though his legs are short
He is always happy as can be
His best friends are you and me!

COLLECTOR'S
VALUE GUIDE™

Value
Totals _____

107

Seamore™
Seal • #4029
Birthdate: December 14, 1996
Issued: June 25, 1994
Retired: October 1, 1997

Original Retail Price: $5-$7
○ Got it! • Paid: $_____
Date Purchased: _____

Market Value:
④-$200 ③-$285 ②-$390
①-$500

*Seamore is a little white seal
Fish and clams are her favorite meal
Playing and laughing in the sand
She's the happiest seal in the land!*

108

Seaweed™
Otter • #4080
Birthdate: March 19, 1996
Issued: January 7, 1996
Current – Moderate To Find

Original Retail Price: $5-$7
○ Got it! • Paid: $_____
Date Purchased: _____

Market Value:
⑤-$_____ ④-$20 ③-$120

*Seaweed is what she likes to eat
It's supposed to be a delicious treat
Have you tried a treat from the water
If you haven't, maybe you "otter"!*

Value
Totals _____

**COLLECTOR'S
VALUE GUIDE™**

Slither™

Snake • #4031
Birthdate: N/A
Issued: June 25, 1994
Retired: June 15, 1995

Original Retail Price: $5-$7
○ Got it! • Paid: $_____
Date Purchased: _____

Market Value:
3–$2,380 **2**–$2,450
1–$2,600

No Poem
_____
_____
_____

109

Sly™

Fox • #4115
Birthdate: September 12, 1996
Issued: June 15, 1996
Current – Easy To Find

Original Retail Price: $5-$7
○ Got it! • Paid: $_____
Date Purchased: _____

Market Value:
A. White belly (Aug. 96–Current)
5–$_____ **4**–$15

B. Brown belly (June 96–Aug. 96)
4–$185

A

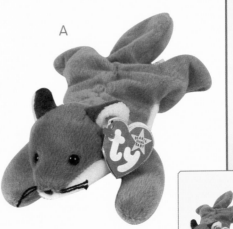

B

110

Sly is a fox and tricky is he
Please don't chase him, let him be
If you want him, just say when
He'll peek out from his den!

111

Smoochy™
Frog • #4039
Birthdate: October 1, 1997
Issued: December 31, 1997
Current – Easy To Find

Original Retail Price: $5-$7
○ Got it! • Paid: $_____
Date Purchased: _____

Market Value:
⑤-$_____

Is he a frog or maybe a prince?
This confusion makes him wince
Find the answer, help him with this
Be the one to give him a kiss!

112

Snip™
Siamese Cat • #4120
Birthdate: October 22, 1996
Issued: January 1, 1997
Current – Easy To Find

Original Retail Price: $5-$7
○ Got it! • Paid: $_____
Date Purchased: _____

Market Value:
⑤-$_____   ④-$15

Snip the cat is Siamese
She'll be your friend if you please
So toss her a toy or a piece of string
Playing with you is her favorite thing!

Value
Totals _____

COLLECTOR'S
VALUE GUIDE™

Snort™

Bull • #4002
Birthdate: May 15, 1995
Issued: January 1, 1997
Current – Easy To Find

Original Retail Price: $5-$7
○ Got it! • Paid: $_____
Date Purchased: _____

Market Value:
⑤-$_____   ④-$10

Although Snort is not so tall
He loves to play basketball
He is a star player in his dreams
Can you guess his favorite team?

Snowball™

Snowman • #4201
Birthdate: December 22, 1996
Issued: October 1, 1997
Retired: December 31, 1997

Original Retail Price: $5-$7
○ Got it! • Paid: $_____
Date Purchased: _____

Market Value:
④-$55

There is a snowman, I've been told
That plays with Beanies out in the cold
What is better in a winter wonderland
Than a Beanie snowman in your hand!

COLLECTOR'S
VALUE GUIDE™

Value
Totals _____

(115)

Sparky™
Dalmatian • #4100
Birthdate: February 27, 1996
Issued: June 15, 1996
Retired: May 11, 1997

Original Retail Price: $5-$7
○ Got it! • Paid: $_____
Date Purchased: _____

Market Value:
❹–$195

*Sparky rides proud on the fire truck
Ringing the bell and pushing his luck
He gets under foot when trying to help
He often gets stepped on and
Lets out a yelp!*

(116)

Speedy™
Turtle • #4030
Birthdate: August 14, 1994
Issued: June 25, 1994
Retired: October 1, 1997

Original Retail Price: $5-$7
○ Got it! • Paid: $_____
Date Purchased: _____

Market Value:
**❹–$45   ❸–$130   ❷–$225
❶–$325**

*Speedy ran marathons in the past
Such a shame, always last
Now Speedy is a big star
After he bought a racing car!*

Value
Totals _____

COLLECTOR'S
VALUE GUIDE™

Spike™

117

Rhinoceros • #4060
Birthdate: August 13, 1996
Issued: June 15, 1996
Current – Moderate To Find

Original Retail Price: $5-$7
◯ Got it! • Paid: **$_____**
Date Purchased: _____

Market Value:
⑤-$_____ ④-$16

Spike the rhino likes to stampede
He's the bruiser that you need
Gentle to birds on his back and spike
You can be his friend if you like!

Spinner™

118

Spider • #4036
Birthdate: October 28, 1996
Issued: October 1, 1997
Current – Moderate To Find

Original Retail Price: $5-$7
◯ Got it! • Paid: **$_____**
Date Purchased: _____

Market Value:
⑤-$_____ ④-$35

Does this spider make you scared?
Among many people that feeling is shared
Remember spiders have feelings too
In fact, this spider really likes you!

COLLECTOR'S
VALUE GUIDE™

Value
Totals _____

Splash™

119

ORIGINAL NINE

Whale • #4022
Birthdate: July 8, 1993
Issued: January 8, 1994
Retired: May 11, 1997

Original Retail Price: $5-$7
○ Got it! • Paid: $_____
Date Purchased: _____

Market Value:
④–**$150** **③**–**$220** **②**–**$295**
①–**$385**

Splash loves to jump and dive
He's the fastest whale alive
He always wins the 100 yard dash
With a victory jump he'll make a splash!

Spooky™

120

A

B

Ghost • #4090
Birthdate: October 31, 1995
Issued: September 1, 1995
Retired: December 31, 1997

Original Retail Price: $5-$7
○ Got it! • Paid: $_____
Date Purchased: _____

Market Value:
A. "Spooky" tag
(Est. Late 95–Dec. 97)
④–**$50** **③**–**$125**

B. "Spook" tag
(Est. Sept. 95–Late 95)
③–**$315**

Ghosts can be a scary sight
But don't let Spooky bring you any fright
Because when you're alone, you will see
The best friend that Spooky can be!

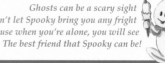

Value
Totals _____

COLLECTOR'S
VALUE GUIDE™

Spot™
Dog • #4000
Birthdate: January 3, 1993
Issued: January 8, 1994
Retired: October 1, 1997

Original Retail Price: $5-$7
◯ Got it! • Paid: $_____
Date Purchased: _____

Market Value:
A. With spot (April 94–Oct. 97)
④–$65 ③–$145 ②–$880

B. Without spot (Jan. 94–April 94)
②–$2,250 ①–$2,400

121

9 ORIGINAL NINE

A

B

See Spot sprint, see Spot run
You and Spot will have lots of fun
Watch out now, because he's not slow
Just stand back and watch him go!

Spunky™
Cocker Spaniel • #4184
Birthdate: January 14, 1997
Issued: December 31, 1997
Current – Moderate To Find

Original Retail Price: $5-$7
◯ Got it! • Paid: $_____
Date Purchased: _____

Market Value:
⑤–$_____

122

Bouncing around without much grace
To jump on your lap and lick your face
But watch him closely he has no fears
He'll run so fast he'll trip over his ears

COLLECTOR'S
VALUE GUIDE™

Value
Totals _____

123

9
ORIGINAL
NINE

Squealer™
Pig • #4005
Birthdate: April 23, 1993
Issued: January 8, 1994
Retired: May 1, 1998

Original Retail Price: $5-$7
○ Got it! • Paid: $_____
Date Purchased: _____

Market Value:
5-$28 **4**-$37 **3**-$120
2-$250 **1**-$350

Squealer likes to joke around
He is known as class clown
Listen to his stories awhile
There is no doubt he'll make you smile!

124

Steg™
Stegosaurus • #4087
Birthdate: N/A
Issued: June 3, 1995
Retired: June 15, 1996

Original Retail Price: $5-$7
○ Got it! • Paid: $_____
Date Purchased: _____

Market Value:
3-$1,050

No Poem
_____
_____
_____
_____

Value
Totals _____

COLLECTOR'S
VALUE GUIDE™

Sting™

(125)

Stingray • #4077
Birthdate: August 27, 1995
Issued: June 3, 1995
Retired: January 1, 1997

Original Retail Price: $5-$7
○ Got it! • Paid: $_____
Date Purchased: _____

Market Value:
④–$250 ③–$320

I'm a manta ray and my name is Sting
I'm quite unusual and this is the thing
Under the water I glide like a bird
Have you ever seen something so absurd?

Stinger™

(126)

NEW!

Scorpion • #4193
Birthdate: September 29, 1997
Issued: May 30, 1998
Current – Just Released

Original Retail Price: $5-$7
○ Got it! • Paid: $_____
Date Purchased: _____

Market Value:
⑤–$_____

Poem Unavailable
_____
_____
_____

COLLECTOR'S
VALUE GUIDE™

| Value Totals | _____ |

127

Stinky™
Skunk • #4017
Birthdate: February 13, 1995
Issued: June 3, 1995
Current – Easy To Find

Original Retail Price: $5-$7
○ Got it! • Paid: $_____
Date Purchased: _____

Market Value:
⑤-$_____   ④-$15   ③-$95

Deep in the woods he lived in a cave
Perfume and mints were the gifts he gave
He showered every night in the kitchen sink
Hoping one day he wouldn't stink!

128

Stretch™
Ostrich • #4182
Birthdate: September 21, 1997
Issued: December 31, 1997
Current – Moderate To Find

Original Retail Price: $5-$7
○ Got it! • Paid: $_____
Date Purchased: _____

Market Value:
⑤-$_____

She thinks when her head is underground
The rest of her body can't be found
The Beanie Babies think it's absurd
To play hide and seek with this bird!

Value
Totals _____

COLLECTOR'S
VALUE GUIDE™

Stripes™

Tiger • #4065
Birthdate: June 11, 1995
Issued: Est. June 3, 1995
Retired: May 1, 1998

Original Retail Price: $5-$7
○ Got it! • Paid: $_____
Date Purchased: _____

A

Market Value:
A. Light w/fewer stripes
   (June 96– May 98)
   ⑤–**$22** ④–**$30**
B. Dark w/fuzzy belly (Est. Early
   96–June 96) ③–**$800**
C. Dark w/more stripes (Est. June
   95–Early 96) ③–**$360**

*Stripes was never fierce nor strong
So with tigers, he didn't get along
Jungle life was hard to get by
So he came to his friends at Ty!*

Strut™

(name changed from "Doodle" in 1997)
Rooster • #4171
Birthdate: March 8, 1996
Issued: July 12, 1997
Current – Moderate To Find

Original Retail Price: $5-$7
○ Got it! • Paid: $_____
Date Purchased: _____

Market Value:
⑤–$_____ ④–**$28**

*Listen closely to "cock-a-doodle-doo"
What's the rooster saying to you?
Hurry, wake up sleepy head
We have lots to do, get out of bed!*

COLLECTOR'S
VALUE GUIDE™

Value
Totals _____

131

Tabasco™
Bull • #4002
Birthdate: May 15, 1995
Issued: June 3, 1995
Retired: January 1, 1997

Original Retail Price: $5-$7
○ Got it! • Paid: $_____
Date Purchased: _____

Market Value:
④-$275 ③-$340

Although Tabasco is not so tall
He loves to play basketball
He is a star player in his dream
Can you guess his favorite team?

132

Tank™
Armadillo • #4031
Birthdate: February 22, 1995
Issued: Est. January 7, 1996
Retired: October 1, 1997

Original Retail Price: $5-$7
○ Got it! • Paid: $_____
Date Purchased: _____

Market Value:
A. 9 plates, with shell
(Est. Late 96–Oct. 97) **④-$90**

B. 9 plates, without shell
(Est. Mid 96–Late 96) **④-$210**

C. 7 plates, without shell
(Est. Jan. 96–Mid 96) **③-$240**

A

B

C

This armadillo lives in the South
Shoving Tex-Mex in his mouth
He sure loves it south of the border
Keeping his friends in good order!

Value
Totals _____

Teddy™ (brown)

Bear • #4050

Birthdate: November 28, 1995
Issued: June 25, 1994
Retired: October 1, 1997

133

Original Retail Price: $5-$7
○ Got it! • Paid: $_____
Date Purchased: _____

Market Value:
A. New face (Jan. 95–Oct. 97)
❹–**$105** ❸–**$275** ❷–**$850**

B. Old face (June 94–Jan. 95)
❷–**$3,400** ❶–**$3,600**

Teddy wanted to go out today
All of his friends went out to play
But he'd rather help whatever you do
After all, his best friend is you!

Teddy™ (cranberry)

134

Bear • #4052
Birthdate: N/A
Issued: June 25, 1994
Retired: January 7, 1996

Original Retail Price: $5-$7
○ Got it! • Paid: $_____
Date Purchased: _____

Market Value:
A. New face (Jan. 95–Jan. 96)
❸–**$2,200** ❷–**$2,300**

B. Old face (June 94–Jan. 95)
❷–**$2,200** ❶–**$2,300**

No Poem
_____
_____
_____
_____

COLLECTOR'S
VALUE GUIDE™

Value
Totals _____

135

A

B

Teddy™ (jade)
Bear • #4057
Birthdate: N/A
Issued: June 25, 1994
Retired: January 7, 1996

Original Retail Price: $5-$7
○ Got it! • Paid: $_____
Date Purchased: _____

Market Value:
A. New face (Jan. 95–Jan. 96)
❸–$2,200 ❷–$2,300

B. Old face (June 94–Jan. 95)
❷–$2,200 ❶–$2,300

No Poem
_____
_____
_____
_____

136

A

B

Teddy™ (magenta)
Bear • #4056
Birthdate: N/A
Issued: June 25, 1994
Retired: January 7, 1996

Original Retail Price: $5-$7
○ Got it! • Paid: $_____
Date Purchased: _____

Market Value:
A. New face (Jan. 95–Jan. 96)
❸–$2,200 ❷–$2,300

B. Old face (June 94–Jan. 95)
❷–$2,100 ❶–$2,200

No Poem
_____
_____
_____

Value
Totals _____

COLLECTOR'S
VALUE GUIDE™

Teddy™ (teal)

137

Bear • #4051
Birthdate: N/A
Issued: June 25, 1994
Retired: January 7, 1996

Original Retail Price: $5-$7
○ Got it! • Paid: $_____
Date Purchased: _____

Market Value:
A. New face (Jan. 95–Jan. 96)
❸–**$2,200** ❷–**$2,300**

B. Old face (June 94–Jan. 95)
❷–**$2,100** ❶–**$2,200**

A

B

No Poem
_____
_____
_____

Teddy™ (violet)

138

Bear • #4055
Birthdate: N/A
Issued: June 25, 1994
Retired: January 7, 1996

Original Retail Price: $5-$7
○ Got it! • Paid: $_____
Date Purchased: _____

Market Value:
A. New face (Jan. 95–Jan. 96)
❸–**$2,200** ❷–**$2,300**

B. Old face (June 94–Jan. 95)
❷–**$2,100** ❶–**$2,200**

A

B

No Poem
_____
_____
_____

COLLECTOR'S
VALUE GUIDE™

Value
Totals _____

139

NEW!

Tracker™
Basset Hound • #4198
Birthdate: June 5, 1997
Issued: May 30, 1998
Current – Just Released

Original Retail Price: $5-$7
○ Got it! • Paid: $_____
Date Purchased: _____

Market Value:
⑤–$_____

Poem Unavailable

_____
_____
_____

140

Trap™
Mouse • #4042
Birthdate: N/A
Issued: June 25, 1994
Retired: June 15, 1995

Original Retail Price: $5-$7
○ Got it! • Paid: $_____
Date Purchased: _____

Market Value:
③–$1,575   ②–$1,650
①–$1,700

No Poem

_____
_____
_____

Value
Totals _____

COLLECTOR'S
VALUE GUIDE™

Tuffy™

Terrier • #4108
Birthdate: October 12, 1996
Issued: May 11, 1997
Current – Easy To Find

Original Retail Price: $5-$7
○ Got it! • Paid: $_____
Date Purchased: _____

Market Value:
⑤-$_____ ④-$13

Taking off with a thunderous blast
Tuffy rides his motorcycle fast
The Beanies roll with laughs and squeals
He never took off his training wheels!

Tusk™

Walrus • #4076
Birthdate: September 18, 1995
Issued: Est. June 3, 1995
Retired: January 1, 1997

Original Retail Price: $5-$7
○ Got it! • Paid: $_____
Date Purchased: _____

Market Value:
④-$195 ③-$270

Tusk brushes his teeth everyday
To keep them shiny, it's the only way
Teeth are special, so you must try
And they will sparkle when
You say "Hi"!

COLLECTOR'S
VALUE GUIDE™

Value
Totals _____

(143)

Twigs™
Giraffe • #4068
Birthdate: May 19, 1995
Issued: January 7, 1996
Retired: May 1, 1998

Original Retail Price: $5-$7
○ Got it! • Paid: $_____
Date Purchased: _____

Market Value:
5-$23 **4**-$30 **3**-$100

Twigs has his head in the clouds
He stands tall, he stands proud
With legs so skinny they wobble and shake
What an unusual friend he will make!

(144)

Valentino™
Bear • #4058
Birthdate: February 14, 1994
Issued: January 7, 1995
Current – Hard To Find

Original Retail Price: $5-$7
○ Got it! • Paid: $_____
Date Purchased: _____

Market Value:
5-$_____ **4**-$35 **3**-$110
2-$205

His heart is red and full of love
He cares for you so give him a hug
Keep him close when feeling blue
Feel the love he has for you!

Value
Totals _____

COLLECTOR'S
VALUE GUIDE™

Velvet™

(145)

Panther • #4064
Birthdate: December 16, 1995
Issued: June 3, 1995
Retired: October 1, 1997

Original Retail Price: $5-$7
○ Got it! • Paid: $_____
Date Purchased: _____

Market Value:
④–$40 ③–$115

Velvet loves to sleep in the trees
Lulled to dreams by the buzz of the bees
She snoozes all day and plays all night
Running and jumping in the moonlight!

Waddle™

(146)

Penguin • #4075
Birthdate: December 19, 1995
Issued: June 3, 1995
Retired: May 1, 1998

Original Retail Price: $5-$7
○ Got it! • Paid: $_____
Date Purchased: _____

Market Value:
⑤–$23 ④–$30 ③–$110

Waddle the Penguin likes to dress up
Every night he wears his tux
When Waddle walks, it never fails
He always trips over his tails!

COLLECTOR'S
VALUE GUIDE™

Value
Totals _____

(147)

Waves™
Whale • #4084
Birthdate: December 8, 1996
Issued: May 11, 1997
Retired: May 1, 1998

Original Retail Price: $5-$7
○ Got it! • Paid: $_____
Date Purchased: _____

Market Value:
5–$23 **4**–$32

Join him today on the Internet
Don't be afraid to get your feet wet
He taught all the Beanies how to surf
Our web page is his home turf!

(148)

Web™
Spider • #4041
Birthdate: N/A
Issued: June 25, 1994
Retired: January 7, 1996

Original Retail Price: $5-$7
○ Got it! • Paid: $_____
Date Purchased: _____

Market Value:
3–$1,700 **2**–$1,850
1–$1,950

No Poem

_____
_____
_____
_____

Value
Totals _____

Weenie™

(149)

Dachshund • #4013
Birthdate: July 20, 1995
Issued: January 7, 1996
Retired: May 1, 1998

Original Retail Price: $5-$7
○ Got it! • Paid: $_____
Date Purchased: _____

Market Value:
5–$25 **4**–$33 **3**–$115

Weenie the dog is quite a sight
Long of body and short of height
He perches himself high on a log
And considers himself to be top dog!

Whisper™

(150)

NEW!

Deer • #4194
Birthdate: April 5, 1997
Issued: May 30, 1998
Current – Just Released

Original Retail Price: $5-$7
○ Got it! • Paid: $_____
Date Purchased: _____

Market Value:
5–$_____

Poem Unavailable
_____
_____
_____

COLLECTOR'S
VALUE GUIDE™

Value
Totals _____

151

NEW!

Wise™
Owl • #4187
Birthdate: May 31, 1997
Issued: May 30, 1998
Current – Just Released

Original Retail Price: $5-$7
○ Got it! • Paid: $_____
Date Purchased: _____

Market Value:
⑤-$_____

With A's and B's he'll always pass
Wise is the head of the class
He's got his diploma and feels really great
Meet the newest graduate: Class of 98!

152

Wrinkles™
Bulldog • #4103
Birthdate: May 1, 1996
Issued: June 15, 1996
Current – Easy To Find

Original Retail Price: $5-$7
○ Got it! • Paid: $_____
Date Purchased: _____

Market Value:
⑤-$_____   ④-$15

This little dog is named Wrinkles
His nose is soft and often crinkles
Likes to climb up on your lap
He's a cheery sort of chap!

Value
Totals _____

COLLECTOR'S
VALUE GUIDE™

Ziggy™

Zebra • #4063
Birthdate: December 24, 1995
Issued: June 3, 1995
Retired: May 1, 1998

Original Retail Price: $5-$7
○ Got it! • Paid: $_____
Date Purchased: _____

Market Value:
5–$23 **4**–$32 **3**–$105

Ziggy likes soccer – he's a referee
That way he watches the games for free
The other Beanies don't think it's fair
But Ziggy the Zebra doesn't care!

Zip™

Cat • #4004
Birthdate: March 28, 1994
Issued: January 7, 1995
Retired: May 1, 1998

Original Retail Price: $5-$7
○ Got it! • Paid: $_____
Date Purchased: _____

A

B

Market Value:
A. White paws (March 96–May 98)
5–$35 **4**–$45 **3**–$575

B. All black (Jan. 96–March 96)
3–$2,250

C. White face (Jan. 95–Jan. 96)
3–$625 **2**–$660

C

Keep Zip by your side all the day through
Zip is good luck, you'll see it's true
When you have something you need to do
Zip will always believe in you!

COLLECTOR'S
VALUE GUIDE™

Value
Totals _____

My Teenie Beanie Babies™ Collection

TB1

Bones™

Dog • 2nd Promotion, #9 of 12
Issued: May 22, 1998
Retired: June 12, 1998

○ Got it! • Paid: $_____
Date Purchased: _____

Market Value: $10

TB2

Bongo™

Monkey • 2nd Promotion, #2 of 12
Issued: May 22, 1998
Retired: June 12, 1998

○ Got it! • Paid: $_____
Date Purchased: _____

Market Value: $15

TB3

Chocolate™

Moose • 1st Promotion, #4 of 10
Issued: April 11, 1997
Retired: May 15, 1997

○ Got it! • Paid: $_____
Date Purchased: _____

Market Value: $30

TB4

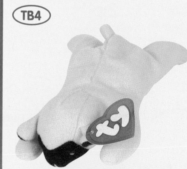

Chops™

Lamb • 1st Promotion, #3 of 10
Issued: April 11, 1997
Retired: May 15, 1997

○ Got it! • Paid: $_____
Date Purchased: _____

Market Value: $35

Value
Totals _____

COLLECTOR'S
VALUE GUIDE™

My Teenie Beanie Babies™ Collection

TB5

Doby™
Doberman • 2nd Promotion, #1 of 12
Issued: May 22, 1998
Retired: June 12, 1998

○ Got it! • Paid: $_____
Date Purchased: _____

Market Value: $15

TB6

Goldie™
Goldfish • 1st Promotion, #5 of 10
Issued: April 11, 1997
Retired: May 15, 1997

○ Got it! • Paid: $_____
Date Purchased: _____

Market Value: $25

TB7

Happy™
Hippo • 2nd Promotion, #6 of 12
Issued: May 22, 1998
Retired: June 12, 1998

○ Got it! • Paid: $_____
Date Purchased: _____

Market Value: $10

TB8

Inch™
Inchworm • 2nd Promotion, #4 of 12
Issued: May 22, 1998
Retired: June 12, 1998

○ Got it! • Paid: $_____
Date Purchased: _____

Market Value: $12

COLLECTOR'S
VALUE GUIDE™

Value
Totals _____

My Teenie Beanie Babies™ Collection

TB9

Lizz™
Lizard • 1st Promotion, #10 of 10
Issued: April 11, 1997
Retired: May 15, 1997

○ Got it! • Paid: $_____
Date Purchased: _____

Market Value: $22

TB10

Mel™
Koala • 2nd Promotion, #7 of 12
Issued: May 22, 1998
Retired: June 12, 1998

○ Got it! • Paid: $_____
Date Purchased: _____

Market Value: $10

TB11

Patti™
Platypus • 1st Promotion, #1 of 10
Issued: April 11, 1997
Retired: May 15, 1997

○ Got it! • Paid: $_____
Date Purchased: _____

Market Value: $40

TB12

Peanut™
Elephant • 2nd Promotion, #12 of 12
Issued: May 22, 1998
Retired: June 12, 1998

○ Got it! • Paid: $_____
Date Purchased: _____

Market Value: $10

Value
Totals _____

COLLECTOR'S
VALUE GUIDE™

TB13

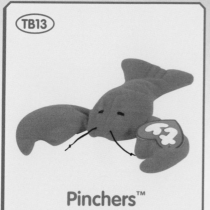

Pinchers™
Lobster • 2nd Promotion, #5 of 12
Issued: May 22, 1998
Retired: June 12, 1998

○ Got it! • Paid: $_____
Date Purchased: _____

Market Value: $10

TB14

Pinky™
Flamingo • 1st Promotion, #2 of 10
Issued: April 11, 1997
Retired: May 15, 1997

○ Got it! • Paid: $_____
Date Purchased: _____

Market Value: $50

TB15

Quacks™
Duck • 1st Promotion, #9 of 10
Issued: April 11, 1997
Retired: May 15, 1997

○ Got it! • Paid: $_____
Date Purchased: _____

Market Value: $20

TB16

Scoop™
Pelican • 2nd Promotion, #8 of 12
Issued: May 22, 1998
Retired: June 12, 1998

○ Got it! • Paid: $_____
Date Purchased: _____

Market Value: $10

COLLECTOR'S
VALUE GUIDE™

Value
Totals _____

My Teenie Beanie Babies™ Collection

TB17

Seamore™

Seal • 1st Promotion, #7 of 10
Issued: April 11, 1997
Retired: May 15, 1997

○ Got it! • Paid: $_____
Date Purchased: _____

Market Value: $25

TB18

Snort™

Bull • 1st Promotion, #8 of 10
Issued: April 11, 1997
Retired: May 15, 1997

○ Got it! • Paid: $_____
Date Purchased: _____

Market Value: $20

TB19

Speedy™

Turtle • 1st Promotion, #6 of 10
Issued: April 11, 1997
Retired: May 15, 1997

○ Got it! • Paid: $_____
Date Purchased: _____

Market Value: $22

TB20

Twigs™

Giraffe • 2nd Promotion, #3 of 12
Issued: May 22, 1998
Retired: June 12, 1998

○ Got it! • Paid: $_____
Date Purchased: _____

Market Value: $12

Value
Totals _____

COLLECTOR'S
VALUE GUIDE™

My Teenie Beanie Babies™ Collection

TB21

Waddle™

Penguin • 2nd Promotion, #11 of 12
Issued: May 22, 1998
Retired: June 12, 1998

○ Got it! • Paid: $_____
Date Purchased: _____

Market Value: $10

TB22

Zip™

Cat • 2nd Promotion, #10 of 12
Issued: May 22, 1998
Retired: June 12, 1998

○ Got it! • Paid: $_____
Date Purchased: _____

Market Value: $10

TB23   '97

**1997 Teenie Beanies
Complete Set (set/10)**

Issued: April 11, 1997
Retired: May 15, 1997

○ Got it! • Paid: $_____
Date Purchased: _____

Market Value: $275

TB24   '98

**1998 Teenie Beanies
Complete Set (set/12)**

Issued: May 22, 1998
Retired: June 12, 1998

○ Got it! • Paid: $_____
Date Purchased: _____

Market Value: $100

COLLECTOR'S
VALUE GUIDE™

Value
Totals _____

Total Value Of My Collection

Value Totals	Value Totals	Value Totals
Page 21	Page 49	Page 77
Page 22	Page 50	Page 78
Page 23	Page 51	Page 79
Page 24	Page 52	Page 80
Page 25	Page 53	Page 81
Page 26	Page 54	Page 82
Page 27	Page 55	Page 83
Page 28	Page 56	Page 84
Page 29	Page 57	Page 85
Page 30	Page 58	Page 86
Page 31	Page 59	Page 87
Page 32	Page 60	Page 88
Page 33	Page 61	Page 89
Page 34	Page 62	Page 90
Page 35	Page 63	Page 91
Page 36	Page 64	Page 92
Page 37	Page 65	Page 93
Page 38	Page 66	Page 94
Page 39	Page 67	Page 95
Page 40	Page 68	Page 96
Page 41	Page 69	Page 97
Page 42	Page 70	Page 98
Page 43	Page 71	Page 99
Page 44	Page 72	Page 100
Page 45	Page 73	Page 101
Page 46	Page 74	Page 102
Page 47	Page 75	Page 103
Page 48	Page 76	
Subtotal	**Subtotal**	**Subtotal**

Grand
Totals _____

COLLECTOR'S
VALUE GUIDE™

*W*hile it was fairly recently that Beanie Babies became a hit, Ty Inc. has been a well-known name among plush lovers for over a decade and some of Ty's other plush animals are becoming "collectible" in their own right.

IT'S RAINING CATS AND DOGS . . .

Having worked for the toy company Dakin upon graduating from college, starting his own company seemed like the next logical step for the entrepreneur Ty Warner. In 1986, Ty established Ty Inc. It all began with a litter of Himalayan cats. Next, Ty expanded its plush line to dogs, bears, a collection of wildlife animals including tigers, frogs, gorillas, elephants and moose, as well as country animals including farm pals, bunnies, cows and even a unicorn.

Then in 1993, Ty introduced the "Attic Treasures Collection," a collection of fully-jointed animals designed to bring a nostalgic element into his growing line-up of plush animals. Originally, these plush pals wore nothing but an occasional ribbon around their neck but around 1996, they became fashion conscious and started appearing in overalls, sweaters and even hats.

In Ty's world, there is something for everyone and in 1995, the company introduced its newest line, "Pillow Pals." Stuffed with a soft, bouncy polyester material (just like a pillow) and with embroidered eyes and noses, these washable critters were designed especially for infants.

With such a wide variety of products, you might be surprised to find that some of your favorite plush pals that aren't Beanie Babies also sport a Ty tag.

*D*o you believe in magic? Because something magical happens when both children and adults meet Beanie Babies. Without a doubt, the Beanie craze that many people predicted wouldn't last is still going – and growing – strong.

It's easy to understand why collectors love Beanie Babies. Who can resist those friendly, little faces and those huggably soft bodies – Beanies make great pals! And because they are relatively inexpensive, kids can usually buy them with their allowances, and several Beanies can be bought at once without taking out a loan!

Ty Inc. never dreamed of the demand it would create when it introduced these cute little critters that were intended to be nothing more than toys. It wasn't long before this demand spiraled out of control and collectors were left trying to track down those Beanies that they could no longer find in their local stores. And that's when they turned to the secondary market.

THE SECONDARY MARKET STORY

With most collectible lines, the secondary market is created when a piece is retired (removed from production) and no longer available in stores. Demand is also created for those rare pieces that feature variations of the piece that was intended to be distributed (see Variations, page 108). For example, the dark blue "Peanut" was a factory mistake and when this was discovered, his fabric was changed to the intended lighter blue. However, as a few of the dark blue elephants did make their way into stores, they became an extremely valuable find and maybe even more rare than the proverbial pink elephant.

While retirements and variations work in a similar way for Beanie Babies, there is an unusual phenomenon that occurs within this line on the secondary market. For many Beanies, a secondary market value is created for even those pieces that are currently in production and, in theory, available at retail price in retail outlets. This may occur for a variety of reasons.

First, as the demand for Beanies is so great, production is often not able to keep up. Consequently, many new releases and hard-to-find pieces are slow to arrive in stores and not readily available, sending collectors into a frenzy to find them. For those not willing to wait for a Beanie that in time will probably reach their local retailer and become available for about $5-$7, the only alternative is to turn to the secondary market where they will pay inflated prices.

Another reason current Beanies may command a high value on the secondary market is the generation tag (see section on Ty tags on page 15). While "Chocolate" the moose may be in every store across America with the currently produced fifth generation hang tag (**5**), his older relative with the second generation tag (**2**) may be a rare and valuable find.

HOW TO ACCESS THE SECONDARY MARKET

There are several ways to access the secondary market. One way is to contact your local retailer who might know of other collectors in the area. Beanie Babies are such a phenomenon that most areas have local swap-and-sells, Beanie stores and kiosks specializing in hard to find Beanies. Another method is through the classified sections of newspapers and collectors' magazines.

With the wonders of the Internet, the world of Beanies will be at your fingertips and you'll be able to find out everything you could possibly want to know about them, from the general to the specific. On-line, you will find sites dedicated to Beanies in which collectors share information and buy, sell and trade pieces. On the web you can also find news and gossip on all types of Beanies. Fortunately, with this wealth of information comes a wealth of options. So the key to successfully buying and selling on the Internet is to take your time and shop around. Ultimately, Beanie Babies will only be worth what collectors are willing to pay for them.

PROTECT YOUR INVESTMENT

One of the most important factors in determining a piece's value on the secondary market is its condition. While they were intended to be played with by children and are quite resilient little critters, Beanies will be most valuable if they are in like-new condition. The "rules" of the Beanie secondary market are that a Beanie should be in perfect condition with its original hang and tush tags still attached. Even Teenie Beanies are more coveted when they remain in their unopened bag. So if your intention is to re-sell your Beanies, it may be a good idea to buy two – one for fun and one for saving.

FOR THE LOVE OF BEANIES

With some of the astronomical prices of Beanie Babies on the secondary market, it is very easy to begin to see collecting them as a financial investment. However, there is no guarantee that a piece will soar in value on the secondary market or that if it does, that the value will continue to stay that high. Remember that Beanie Babies were introduced as toys, intended for the sole purpose of bringing a smile to the faces of all that see them. Therefore, the best reason to collect these bean-filled pals is for the fun and happiness that they inspire.

V ariation is the spice of life and some Beanie lovers might be inclined to agree. While some collectors are content with adding new releases to their treasure troves, others will not rest until they have all of the Beanie Babies, in all of their various incarnations. These selective souls will go to swap-and-sells, comb the want ads and post millions of messages on the Internet, all in the hope of locating an all-black "Zip" the cat or a gray "Happy" the hippo These collectors revel in the world of Beanie variations!

The secondary market activity for Beanie Babies is already brisk, especially on the Internet, but the Beanie hunt goes to a whole new level when variations are considered. For example, the wingless "Quackers" or the spotless "Spot" command top dollar, while other variations are more of a curiosity and will increase the price of the affected Beanie Babies marginally, if at all.

WHO'S WHO?

"Rainbow"

Color changes, name changes and physical design changes serve to create many new and wonderful Beanies! There are also variations in the hang tags and tush tags attached to each Beanie design. In some cases, the tags have mistakenly been attached to the wrong Beanie, as was the case of the multi-colored "Rainbow" and the blue-gray "Iggy," or with the "Waves" and "Echo" switch (neither instance has seen a significant secondary market increase, though some collectors do seek them out). Finally, there are some discrepancies between the tags themselves, often in the names (such as "Tuck" instead of "Tusk," and "Punchers" instead of "Pinchers"), the birthdates and the poems.

"Iggy"

It can be very satisfying to come across the variation that you've been looking to add to your collection but you must know something about what you are buying. To lessen the possibility of being roped into purchasing a counterfeit, you should walk away from a deal without opening your wallet if you are uncertain about a piece!

On the next few pages are some of the common, and not-so-common, variations out there.

NAME CHANGES

Brownie™/Cubbie™ . . . "Cubbie" was first introduced in 1994 as "Brownie." If your bear doesn't have "Cubbie" on his two tags, you're the lucky owner of the earlier "Brownie."

Doodle™/Strut™ . . . "Doodle" the rooster dawdled out of the collection – rumor has it, after a copyright issue with another company – at which point "Strut" strolled in.

Maple™ . . . This Canadian bear was initially named "Pride," up until a last-minute name change. As a result, some "Maple" bears made it into the market with the name "Pride" on the tush tags.

Nana™/Bongo™ . . . "Bongo" the monkey was introduced as "Nana," a brown monkey with a tan tail. After the name change, "Bongo" has appeared with both a brown and a tan tail.

Spooky™ . . . Early in the production of this scary creature, there were several ghostly sightings of "Spooky" with tags that read "Spook." After debuting in September 1995, "Spook" was only available for a few months before his name changed.

COLOR CHANGES

Digger™ . . . "Digger" the crab was first produced as an orange crab but he must have spent one too many days in the sun because he soon appeared a shade of bright red.

Happy™ . . . It must have been a "Happy" day when this hippo changed from the basic "hippo gray" to a new lavender hue. The gray version is now very coveted on the secondary market.

Inky™ . . . "Inky" the octopus first appeared as a tan creature, but he soon lightened up and started appearing in stores as a pleasant shade of pink. During his months as "the tan Inky," this creature of the sea was occasionally seen without a mouth.

Lizzy™ . . . "Lizzy" the lizard likes to buck the current trend. When she was introduced she wore a tie-dyed outfit, but now that tie-dye is so popular, "Lizzy" has moved on to a different look. The more recent (but now retired) "Lizzy" wears a sleek blue top with black spots that is paired with a yellow bottom with an orange reptile print.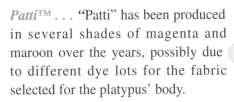

Patti™ . . . "Patti" has been produced in several shades of magenta and maroon over the years, possibly due to different dye lots for the fabric selected for the platypus' body.

Peanut™ . . . When "Peanut" was initially introduced the intention was that the she would be made in sky blue but she appeared as a royal blue elephant instead. About 2,000 "Peanuts" were made before the switch to lighter blue.

DESIGN CHANGES

Derby™ and Mystic™. . . . These two Beanie Babies each came with their manes and tails made out of fine and coarse yarn. More recently, a white spot, known as a "star," has been added to the center of "Derby" the horse's forehead, while an iridescent horn has replaced the tan horn on "Mystic" the unicorn.

Inch™ . . . Inch by inch, this little inchworm helps the garden grow. First appearing with felt antennas, "Inch" now sports black yarn antennas.

Lucky™ . . . "Lucky" the ladybug can be found in several renditions. She was first released with seven felt spots glued to her shiny red shell. She later appeared on the scene wearing a brand new shell with printed spots

that were part of the fabric. "Lucky" with printed spots has been found with approximately 11 spots and, in a rarer version, around 21 spots.

Magic™ . . . "Magic" the dragon has a flair for drama. She was originally released with pale pink thread decorating her iridescent wings. The thread was later changed to a hot pink. The change to the brighter thread was a short one though, and soon she had reverted back to the light pink stitching.

Nip™ and Zip™ . . . It's hard to tell who is the trendsetter and who is the copycat between "Nip" and "Zip." These two cats have both been through three incarnations, but in different hues. ("Nip" has a gold coat, while "Zip" has a black coat.) First they appeared with a white face and belly, then both went to a solid color, and finally the pair ended up with little white booties on their front and back paws.

Quackers™ . . . When "Quackers" was introduced in 1994 he was, well, aerodynamically challenged because the poor duck was without wings. Redesigned shortly after his release, the new and improved "Quackers" featured a sleek, winged body that was ready for take-off.

Sly™ . . . "Sly" has always been a shy fox that liked to hug the shadows with his dark brown body. But as "Sly" got older, he got a wee bit bolder, and asked for a white belly. No longer camouflaged, he's easier to see.

Spot™ . . . With a name like "Spot," one might reasonably expect the dog to be spotted! But "Spot" was spot-less when he was originally introduced. When astute consumers pointed this fact out, Ty obligingly came out with another version.

VARIATIONS

Stripes™ . . . "Stripes" has been spotted with three variations. Originally released in a dark orange and black striped fabric, "Stripes" can also be found in a lighter gold, with wider spaces between the black stripes. Some of the "Stripes" with the darker fabric were produced with a fuzzy belly.

Tank™ . . . Although armadillos haven't changed much over the past million years, this armadillo has evolved quite a bit since it was introduced in 1996. "Tank" was first issued with 7 lines on his back, then 9, and is now featured with a more defined shell thanks to horizontal stitches added to his sides. Also, the armadillo's ears are now on the top of his head, rather than at the sides as they once were.

Teddy™ . . . A group of six colorful bears named "Teddy" were introduced in 1994 with their eyes near the outside of their faces and smaller, pointed noses. The brown, cranberry, jade, magenta, teal and violet "Teddy" bears all underwent "face-lifts" and ended up with their eyes closer to the middle of their faces and with shorter, rounder snouts.

*D*o you or any of your friends share a birthday with any of your favorite Beanie Babies?

JANUARY

Jan. 3, 1993 . . . . Spot™
Jan. 5, 1997 . . . . Kuku™
Jan. 6, 1993 . . . . Patti™
Jan. 13, 1996 . . . . Crunch™
Jan. 14, 1997 . . . . Spunky™
Jan. 15, 1996 . . . . Mel™
Jan. 18, 1994 . . . . . Bones™
Jan. 21, 1996 . . . . . . Nuts™
Jan. 25, 1995 . . . . Peanut™
Jan. 26, 1996 . . . . . . Chip™

FEBRUARY

Feb. 1, 1996 . . . . . . Peace™
Feb. 4, 1997 . . . . . . Fetch™
Feb. 13, 1995 . . . . . Stinky™
Feb. 13, 1995 . . . . . . Pinky™
Feb. 14, 1994 . . Valentino™
Feb. 17, 1996 . . . . . . Baldy™
Feb. 20, 1996 . . . . . Roary™
Feb. 20, 1997 . . . . . . Early™
Feb. 22, 1995 . . . . . . Tank™
Feb. 25, 1994 . . . . Happy™
Feb. 27, 1996 . . . . Sparky™
Feb. 28, 1995 . . . . Flip™

MARCH

March 2, 1995 . . . . . Coral™
March 6, 1994 . . . . . . Nip™
March 7, 1997 . . . . . . Gigi™
March 8, 1996 . . . Doodle™
March 8, 1996 . . . . . Strut™
March 12, 1997 . . . Rocket™
March 14, 1994 . . . . . Ally™
March 17, 1997 . . . . . . Erin™
March 19, 1996 . . Seaweed™
March 21, 1996 . . . Fleece™
March 28, 1994 . . . . . Zip™

APRIL

April 3, 1996 . . . . Hoppity™
April 4, 1997 . . . . . . Hissy™
April 5, 1997 . . . . Whisper™
April 12, 1996 . . . . . . Curly™
April 16, 1997 . . . . . . Jake™
April 18, 1995 . . . . . . Ears™
April 19, 1994 . . . Quackers™
April 23, 1993 . . Squealer™
April 25, 1993 . . . . . . Legs™
April 27, 1993 . . . Chocolate™

MAY

May 1, 1995 . . . . . . Lucky™
May 1, 1996 . . . . Wrinkles™
May 2, 1996 . . . . . Pugsly™
May 3, 1996 . . . . . . Chops™
May 10, 1994 . . . . . Daisy™
May 11, 1995 . . . . . Lizzy™
May 13, 1993 . . . . . . Flash™
May 15, 1995 . . . . . . Snort™
May 15, 1995 . . . Tabasco™
May 19, 1995 . . . . . Twigs™
May 21, 1994 . . . . . Mystic™
May 28, 1996 . . . Floppity™
May 30, 1996 . . . . . Rover™
May 31, 1997 . . . . . . Wise™

JUNE

June 1, 1996 . . . . . Hippity™
June 3, 1996 . . . . Freckles™
June 3, 1996 . . . . . Scottie™
June 5, 1997 . . . . Tracker™
June 8, 1995 . . . . . Bucky™
June 8, 1995 . . . . . Manny™
June 11, 1995 . . . . . Stripes™
June 15, 1996 . . . . Scottie™
June 17, 1996 . . . . Gracie™
June 19, 1993 . . . Pinchers™
June 27, 1995 . . . . Bessie™

BEANIE BABIES® BIRTHDAYS

JULY

July 1, 1996 . . . . . . Maple™
July 1, 1996 . . . . . . Scoop™
July 2, 1995 . . . . . Bubbles™
July 4, 1996 . . . . Lefty™
July 4, 1996 . . . . . . Righty™
July 4, 1997 . . . . Glory™
July 8, 1993 . . . . . . Splash™
July 14, 1995 . . . . . . Ringo™
July 15, 1994 . . . . Blackie™
July 19, 1995 . . . . . Grunt™
July 20, 1995 . . . . Weenie™
July 28, 1996 . . . . Freckles™

AUGUST

Aug. 1, 1995 . . . . . Garcia™
Aug. 9, 1995 . . . . . . Hoot™
Aug. 12, 1997 . . . . . . Iggy™
Aug. 13, 1996 . . . . . Spike™
Aug. 14, 1994 . . . Speedy™
Aug. 17, 1995 . . . . Bongo™
Aug. 17, 1995 . . . . . Nana™
Aug. 23, 1995 . . . . Digger™
Aug. 27, 1995 . . . . . Sting™
Aug. 28, 1997 . . . Pounce™

SEPTEMBER

Sept. 3, 1995 . . . . Inch™
Sept. 3, 1996 . . . . Claude™
Sept. 5, 1995 . . . . . Magic™
Sept. 9, 1997 . . . . . Bruno™
Sept. 12, 1996 . . . . Sly™
Sept. 16, 1995 . . . . Derby™
Sept. 16, 1995 . . . . . . Kiwi™
Sept. 18, 1995 . . . . . . Tusk™
Sept. 21, 1997 . . . . Stretch™
Sept. 29, 1997 . . . Stinger™

OCTOBER

Oct. 1, 1997 . . . . Smoochy™
Oct. 3, 1996 . . . . . . Bernie™
Oct. 9, 1996 . . . . . . Doby™
Oct. 10, 1997 . . . . Jabber™
Oct. 12, 1996 . . . . . . Tuffy™
Oct. 14, 1997 . . Rainbow™
Oct. 16, 1995 . . . . Bumble™
Oct. 17, 1996 . . . . . . Dotty™
Oct. 22, 1996 . . . . . . Snip™
Oct. 28, 1996 . . . . Spinner™
Oct. 29, 1996 . . . . . Batty™
Oct. 30, 1995 . . . . . Radar™
Oct. 31, 1995 . . . . Spooky™

NOVEMBER

Nov. 3, 1997 . . . . . . Puffer™
Nov. 6, 1996 . . . . . Pouch™
Nov. 7, 1997 . . . . Ants™
Nov. 9, 1996 . . . . . Congo™
Nov. 14, 1993 . . . . Cubbie™
Nov. 14, 1994 . . . . Goldie™
Nov. 20, 1997 . . . . Prance™
Nov. 21, 1996 . . . . Nanook™
Nov. 27, 1996 . . . Gobbles™
Nov. 28, 1995 . Teddy™ (brown)
Nov. 29, 1994 . . . . . . Inky™

DECEMBER

Dec. 2, 1996 . . . . Jolly™
Dec. 6, 1997 . . . . Fortune™
Dec. 8, 1996 . . . . . Waves™
Dec. 12, 1996 . . . Blizzard™
Dec. 14, 1996 . . Seamore™
Dec. 15, 1997 . . Britannia™
Dec. 16, 1995 . . . . . Velvet™
Dec. 19, 1995 . . . . Waddle™
Dec. 21, 1996 . . . . . . Echo™
Dec. 22, 1996 . . Snowball™
Dec. 24, 1995 . . . . . Ziggy™
Dec. 25, 1996 . 1997 Teddy™

WORD SEARCH

Find your favorite Beanie Babies® in this challenging word search.
There are 17 in all. Happy hunting! (See page 125 for answers.)

```
D K S K B W B S F O B L
W M G I G I S G L M E B
B H N O H C T E F P K L
Q X I Z P X I L N P A S
P I N S N O N B X B J C
R U N P P L G M K N O P
E Y L R A E E Q F U X B
B A G E G L R M O G K C
B R O C K E T B R L N U
A L L Y K L Z E T O R S
J U M C B R T S U R P L
P N A N T S Z I N Y B R
L R M N B C D W E L Q S
T O P X M N W V Y M P Q
```

ALLY™
ANTS™
EARLY™
FETCH™
FORTUNE™
GLORY™
GIGI™
JABBER™
JAKE™
KUKU™
LEGS™
ROCKET™
SNIP™
STINGER™
TRACKER™
WHISPER™
WISE™

WORD SCRAMBLE

Rearrange the letters to spell your favorite Beanie Babies® names.
The yellow boxes spell out a Secret Beanie's name. Good luck!
(See page 125 for answers.)

1. EBJABR
2. SCISEPNR
3. EIBSES
4. AKTERCR
5. DWEESAE
6. ITRESNG
7. ENFUORT
8. SPHWERI
9. YORRA

" I LOVE THE WATER, WHO AM I ? "

SECRET BEANIE

FUN & GAMES

WHAT'S WRONG WITH THIS PICTURE?
How many things can you find wrong with this picture?
(See page 125 for answers.)

TRIVIA QUIZ
Test your knowledge of Beanie Babies® facts here!
(See page 125 for answers.)

1. Of the "Original Nine" Beanie Babies, which ones are still current?

2. One of the Beanie Babies shares his name with a famous actor, who was born Rudolpho d'Antonguolla. Name the Beanie Baby and the actor.

3. Which Beanie Babies have flags on their bodies?

4. In 1997, Ty teamed up with a Major League Baseball team for the first Beanie Babies giveaway. Name the Beanie and the baseball team.

5. Name the two 1997 Teenie Beanies and their larger Beanie Babies counterparts whose names do not match.

Congratulations to everyone who has entered Collectors' Publishing's Dream Beanie Contest. Here are the winners for the months of February, March, April and May. New winners are announced monthly. See the last page of the book for details on how you can enter!

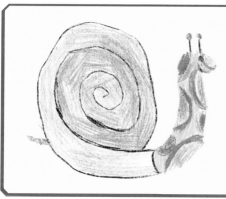

1ST PLACE WINNER
Slugger
THE SNAIL
BIRTHDAY: JANUARY 1, 1998

By: Hilary H.
Hometown: Fredericksburg, VA

This little snail slugs along,
Singing his happy little song.
Wishing luck throughout the year,
Hoping that you will keep him near.

2ND PLACE WINNER
Chipper
THE GRASSHOPPER
BIRTHDAY: MAY 17, 1998

By: Anne G.
Hometown: Biddeford, ME

I'll hop into your heart,
Right from the very start.
'Cause I'm a chipper guy,
And I can even fly.

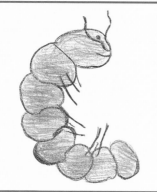

3RD PLACE WINNER
Sherman
THE SHRIMP
BIRTHDAY: MARCH 3, 1998

By: Margaret W.
Hometown: Brownsville, TN

Sherman the shrimp loves to swim,
He also loves for you to play with him.
And so I guess that is why,
He decided to come to Ty.

1ST PLACE WINNER
Sunny
THE GECKO
BIRTHDAY: JULY 21, 1998

By: Kaia T.
Hometown: Renton, WA

Sunny the gecko lives in a tree,
He hides in the leaves so he's hard to see.
He moves his eyes from left to right,
So he can get a tasty bite.

2ND PLACE WINNER
Pearl
THE OYSTER
BIRTHDAY: APRIL 16, 1998

By: Dana H.
Hometown: Chesapeake, VA

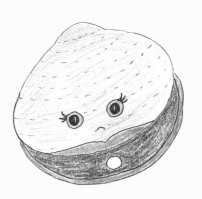

Pearl the oyster is so sweet,
She's the nicest oyster you'll ever meet.
In her shell, a gem is found,
She made it herself, perfectly round.

3RD PLACE WINNER
Slimy
THE SLUG
BIRTHDAY: MAY 9, 1998

By: Cindy L.
Hometown: Churchton, MD

My name is Slimy, I travel at night,
I like to eat before daylight.
A trail is left wherever I go,
And my speed is oh so slow.

1ST PLACE WINNER
Colors
THE PEACOCK
BIRTHDAY: APRIL 12, 1998

By: Kirstin O.
Hometown: Bradenton, FL

Whenever Colors goes out,
She always acts like a girl scout.
Walking straight, walking proud,
She always makes a big crowd.

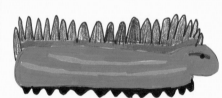

2ND PLACE WINNER
Fuzz
THE CATERPILLAR
BIRTHDAY: SEPTEMBER 29, 1997

By: Katy S.
Hometown: Bothell, WA

Fuzz loves to eat leaves and stems,
He owns a lovely collection of gems.
Fuzz tickles your hand when he walks,
But he hardly ever talks.

3RD PLACE WINNER
Gregory Peck
THE WOODPECKER
BIRTHDAY: AUGUST 1

By: Morgan F.
Hometown: Jonesboro, AR

Gregory the "peck" lives in a tree,
Pecking for things he can't even see.
His wings are what carry him around,
But his beak makes his drilling sound.

1ST PLACE WINNER
Nevermore

THE RAVEN
BIRTHDAY: MARCH 1, 1998

By: Sarah S.
Hometown: St. Joseph, MO

This raven you see sits in a tree,
Figuring out puzzles like you and me.
If you ask him if life is a bore,
He simply says, "Nevermore."

2ND PLACE WINNER
Bristles

THE HEDGEHOG
BIRTHDAY: APRIL 17, 1998

By: Elizabeth W.
Hometown: North Providence, RI

This hedgehog's name is Bristles,
He lives among the thistles.
He's a country lad and quite content,
To live underground and to pay no rent.

3RD PLACE WINNER
Crockie

THE CROCODILE
BIRTHDAY: APRIL 4, 1998

By: Russell P.
Hometown: Middletown, OH

Crockie likes to bask in the sun,
He goes in the swamp to have some fun.
Don't turn your back when he's around,
Cause if he nips you, you'll wear a frown.

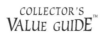

INDEX BY ANIMAL TYPE

Below is an alphabetical listing of the Beanies and the pages you can find them on in the Value Guide!

GAMES ANSWERS

WORD SEARCH

WORD SCRAMBLE
1. Jabber™
2. Princess™
3. Bessie™
4. Tracker™
5. Seaweed™
6. Stinger™
7. Fortune™
8. Whisper™
9. Roary™
secret Beanie:
Britannia™

WHAT'S WRONG WITH THIS PICTURE
1. moon 2. pineapple in tree 3. missing sneaker 4. upside down ice cream cone 5. empty ice cream cone on sign 6. misspelling on sign 7. house on sign 8. shoe on sign 9. banana on sign 10. bowling ball on sign 11. missing headlight 12. upside down roof 13. dice without dots 14. square tire 15. license plate mistake.

TRIVIA QUIZ
1. Only "Chocolate" the moose is still current. 2. "Valentino" the bear and Rudolph Valentino, the famous actor of the 1920s. 3. "Britannia," "Glory," "Lefty," "Libearty," "Maple" and "Righty." 4. "Cubbie" the bear and the Chicago Cubs. 5. "Lizz" and "Lizzy," "Quacks" and "Quackers."

Look for these other

COLLECTOR'S
VALUE GUIDE™

titles at fine gift and collectible stores everywhere.

The
BOYDS COLLECTION LTD.

Department 56®
Villages

Cherished
Teddies®
by ENESCO®

Department 56®
Snowbabies©

HARBOUR
LIGHTS®

HALLMARK
Keepsake Ornaments

Dreamsicles™

Precious
Moments®
by ENESCO

Also from Collectors' Publishing . . .

Charming
Tails

SWAROVSKI
Silver Crystal

BEANIE BOX™

• U.V. PROTECTION – STOPS FADING
• REVERSIBLE BACKDROP
  – VERTICAL OR HORIZONTAL
• STACKABLE – EASY TO DISPLAY

BEANIE I.D.
TAG
PROTECTORS™

PROTECTS THE HEART TAG!

• WITH "I BELONG TO" I.D. TAGS
• COMES IN SIX DIFFERENT COLORS

HARMONY
KINGDOM

COLLECTORS'
PUBLISHING
www.collectorspub.com

COLLECTORS' PUBLISHING
PRESENTS THE
DREAM BEANIE
CONTEST

SEND YOUR ENTRY TO:
COLLECTORS' PUBLISHING
P.O. BOX 2333
MERIDEN, CT 06450

Here's How You Enter:

Use your imagination to dream up your very own "Dream Beanie." *PICK A NAME.* **CREATE A BIRTHDATE. WRITE A POEM. DRAW A PICTURE.** Monthly winners will be posted on our website (www.collectorspub.com) and a lucky few will get published in future editions of the Collector's Value Guide™ and/or other publications. Enter as many times as you wish by copying this form or using your own white, unlined sheet of paper. Maybe your Beanie will enter Collectors' Publishing's Dream Beanie Hall Of Fame! Good luck and have fun!!!

SHARE YOUR DREAM BEANIE IDEAS WITH COLLECTOR FRIENDS!

Your Name _____

Address _____
          Street Address

_____
Town   State   Zip

Phone _____

*FOR KIDS!!!
FOR ADULTS!!!*

STORE WHERE YOU BUY YOUR BEANIES:

Store Name _____

Town & State _____

SCHOOLKIDS:

Age & Grade _____

School Name _____

Town & State _____

MAYBE YOUR DREAM BEANIE WILL BE A WINNER!

Contest Rules:

No purchase necessary. All submissions become the property of Collectors' Publishing. Collectors' Publishing is not affiliated with Ty Inc. and winning designs will not be produced by Ty. Winners will be selected by the Collectors' Publishing staff. Due to the volume of entries, we cannot respond to all entries and submissions are not returnable. All entries must be postmarked no later than December 31, 1998. For a list of winners, write to Collectors' Publishing, Attn: Contest Winners, P.O. Box 2333, Meriden, CT 06450 or check our website at **www.collectorspub.com**. Void where prohibited by law.

**COLLECTORS'
PUBLISHING**

COLLECTORS' PUBLISHING

PRESENTS THE

DREAM BEANIE CONTEST

SEND YOUR ENTRY TO:
COLLECTORS' PUBLISHING
P.O. BOX 2333
MERIDEN, CT 06450

MY DREAM BEANIE IS A (ANIMAL TYPE):

_____

MY DREAM BEANIE'S NAME IS:

_____

MY DREAM BEANIE'S BIRTHDATE IS:

_____

MY DREAM BEANIE'S POEM IS:

_____

_____

_____

_____

MY DREAM BEANIE LOOKS LIKE THIS: